The Complete Reiki Course

Master Naharo with **Gail Radford**

The Complete

Reiki Course

Astrolog ◆ The Quality of Life Series ◆

Series editor: Sara Bleich
Editor: Marion Duman
Cover design: Na'ama Yaffe
Layout and Graphics: Ruth Erez
Illustrations: Arava Sheleff
Photographs: Ofer Ben Mordechai
Model: Sivan Prag
Production Manager: Dan Gold

ISBN 9654941198

Published by Astrolog Publishing House 2001

Astrolog Publishing House
P. O. Box 1123, Hod Hasharon 45111, Israel
Tel: 972-9-7412044
Fax: 972-9-7442714

E-Mail: info@astrolog.co.il

Printed in Israel

1 3 5 7 9 10 8 6 4 2

Contents

Introduction

When I (Gail) met Master Naharo for the first time, we were both in Calcutta. He was on a lecture tour during which he administered Reiki treatments (free of charge!) to the city's poor, and I was on a journey of spiritual purification. The first time I visited Calcutta, I was stunned by the poverty of the huge city, by the unbearably awful smell that dominates it, by the hopelessness that gnaws at its every corner. I fled. I fled from the city that is unbearable to the senses, preferring the beauty spots of vast India. Now I had returned to purify my soul. I asked myself in what way I was better than the fifteen million who lived in Calcutta. I actually learned to see the pearls hidden in the sewage and the dirt... and I met Master Naharo for the first time.

"I can give you the gift of Reiki orally," he laughed when I asked him what Reiki meant and how I could acquire it. "Reiki is like a magic wand – the moment you hold it, you can reach the Reiki sources, feel the energy that is flowing within you, and use it to perform 'miracles.' Here, read this."

He handed me a sheet of paper with two columns of print on it – one column in English and the second in the language spoken in India, which I could not read, but whose letters I was familiar with. That sheet contained the principles of Reiki, five in number.

"The fact is, if you read and accept these principles, you can be a Reiki practitioner, a Reiki therapist or a Reiki Master. Everything is inside you," he said slightly derisively.

"That's not what I've heard," I told him. "There are Reiki courses for which the teachers take substantial fees, and receiving Reiki involves receiving initiation from the teacher and acquiring a set of mysterious symbols, not to mention special treatment techniques and weird and wonderful 'professional secrets'..."

"That's true," said Master Naharo. "But look at it in this way..." He pointed at a group of babies crawling/climbing up a hillock of sand in the park where we were standing. "Those infants are busy climbing a hill without equipment or expert knowledge. It's the same with mountain-climbers who have both experience and knowledge, who are equipped with the most expensive gear in the world, climbing the peaks of Nepal. What's the difference? Both the former and the latter climb! But it is clear to me, as it is to you, that knowledge, experience, and equipment all enhance the ability to climb, and the hill of sand becomes the loftiest of mountains. This is exactly what happens in Reiki, too. Every person can resemble the baby climbing the hill of sand. But only the person who knows and is familiar with Reiki, who has delved into it and learned its symbols and methods, can reach the peak of the lofty mountain."

I did not experience Reiki on that occasion. It was only a few months later, when I reached Poonah, that I joined Master Naharo's pupils and began my journey along the path of Reiki.

This book, which was written with the inspiration and supervision of Master Naharo, is the mountain peak I reached.

When I examined, together with Master Naharo and other pupils, the possibility of disseminating the blessing of Reiki throughout the world, I had the idea of compiling a set of lessons in the form of a textbook, at the end of which the reader could test himself and take the Reiki "exam," which would culminate in the conferral of a qualifying diploma. Very few people supported me in the implementation of this idea; the conventional belief was that initiation was the basis for receiving Reiki. However, Master Naharo's support was overridingly important, and the moment I received his blessing, I got down to work.

"This book must be a complete course with which the pupil or reader will be able to perform self-initiation," the Master instructed me. "It is important that the reader not need you, me or any other teacher – everything must be in the book: the explanations, principles, symbols, hand placements, treatment points, treatment methods... Do you realize that after the publication of this book, people will be able to train themselves in Reiki without any need for teachers?"

That is precisely the aim of this book.

The Complete Reiki Course is divided into three parts:

The first part, "Lessons in Reiki," is the theoretical part, which tells about Reiki and explains its principles, its method of treatment, and its contribution to mankind. At the end of this part, the reader who has internalized its contents is permitted to confer upon himself a diploma testifying to his status as a Reiki I practitioner.

The second part, "Reiki Exercises," is the practical, "technical" part of Reiki – symbols, hand placements, and treatment methods. In this part of the book, the stress is on clarity, and we have added diagrams and photos wherever possible. At the end of this part, the reader-practitioner can confer upon himself a diploma testifying to his status as a Reiki II practitioner.

The third part contains "appendices" – a full explanation of the Marma points, which are suitable for therapy and healing by means of Reiki, as well as a chapter that elaborates on the nature of the chakras and their importance, and a chapter in which meditation (an important tool during Reiki) is discussed.

Our blessings go with you on this fascinating journey to Reiki energy, and we hope to hear about your success along the Reiki path upon which you are starting.

Master Naharo

Gail

PART 1

Lessons in Reiki

The Beginning of Modern Reiki

The wonderful story of Reiki begins in mid-nineteenth-century Japan. It is a story that transcends continents, religions, and races, and its origins reside in the obstinate search for the special healing treatment by touch, which is hinted at in ancient writings. At the time, Dr. Mikao Usui was the dean of a small Christian university in Kyoto. That period was a period of change in Japanese life, which began to be exposed to Western culture. The innovations of the Industrial Revolution in the West rapidly began to make their mark in Japan. Dr. Mikao Usui was intimately acquainted with one aspect of western culture: Christianity.

His belief in the Bible and the holy scriptures was so profound that while teaching his students the Bible and the New Testament, they asked him if he accepted the holy scriptures in letter and spirit. "Of course," he answered, continuing to read the healing miracles wrought by Jesus with his students. "If that is the case," his students went on, "where is that hidden power by means of which Jesus and his disciples performed far-reaching medical miracles? Where is that power?" Since Dr. Usui could not provide a satisfactory answer to his students' questions, he felt that it was his personal obligation to set out on a quest for the answers. The very day he was asked the questions, he resigned from his post, and went off in search of the answers to the astonishing questions.

Initially, Dr. Usui went to the United States, because most of his teachers were American missionaries. He thought that perhaps by a meticulous scrutiny of the Christian scriptures, he would discover the answers. However, he did not find any answers there either. When it occurred to him that Buddha, too, had far-reaching medical abilities, he decided to return to Japan, where he would try to find the answers to his questions: What are the marvelous divine healing powers described in the scriptures and in the stories about Buddha, and how is it possible to link up to them and bring them back into this world for the benefit of the suffering and the oppressed?

Dr. Usui commenced a thorough search among the Buddhist monasteries in Japan. He searched in the ancient Buddhist sutras, asked the abbots and monks in the monasteries, but always, whenever he requested information, material or any kind of clues about Buddha's ways of healing the body, he received the same answer: over time, healing work had become focused on the spirit only, and no documentation concerning Buddha's marvelous methods of treating and healing the body was to be found. This answer did not satisfy Dr. Usui. In the New Testament, as well as in the Bible, cases of healing the suffering body itself were described. The same was true in the numerous stories about

Buddha. Where were all those ancient methods? How could they be accessed? And so Dr. Usui continued his search.

Although he had plenty of reasons to give up after trying so many different places, and after asking so many abbots and sages and not receiving any answers, his spirit was not broken. He continued searching until he reached an isolated Zen monastery, from which he received a little bit of encouragement. The venerable abbot was not surprised at Dr. Usui's questions. He even agreed with him. Buddha had indeed been gifted with the ability to heal people's bodies. The fascinating question also intrigued the old abbot, who suggested that Dr. Usui stay in the monastery and continue his marvelous quest there by reading the sutras and the ancient Japanese texts. His support heartened Dr. Usui, and strengthened his spirit; his courage was bolstered. However, even in the ancient Japanese texts, he was unable to find the answers to his questions.

He began to search in the ancient Chinese sutras, and by dint of the tremendous power of learning and research with which he was blessed, rapidly covered a substantial part of the contents of the ancient sutras that he managed to lay his hands on. Even in these sutras, however, Dr. Usui succeeded in finding very little information. He still refused to give up. Now he hoped to find the answer in the ancient Tibetan sutras. To that end, he had to learn Sanskrit, the ancient language in which the Tibetan sutras were written.

It seems that during the time Dr. Usui went on his wonderful journey to northern India, to the Himalayas, ancient scrolls containing extremely valuable information were discovered there. We do not know if Dr. Usui actually got hold of those scrolls, but after the journey and after learning the Tibetan lotus sutras, Dr. Usui felt that he had the information, the intellectual answer, to his questions. This was not enough, of course. In order to heal with the help of these marvelous powers, he needed the inspiration of a superior force, a divine blessing.

Armed with his new knowledge, Dr. Usui returned to his friend, the abbot, with a new question: How is it possible to receive these powers and use them for the benefit of mankind? The two friends meditated together for a long time in an attempt to receive an answer to the question. Finally, they realized that the only way was for Dr. Usui to undertake a journey to the holy mountain, Mt. Kuri-Yama, in the vicinity of Kyoto, where he would undertake a regime of fasting and meditation for 21 days.

Dr. Usui climbed the mountain. He reached a certain point, which faced east, and there he arranged a formation of 21 stones, each one indicating a day of fasting and meditation. By the time he reached the 21st stone, nothing special or extraordinary had happened yet. It was the time of the new moon, and the mountain was virtually in darkness. Dr. Usui prayed with all his heart for a divine answer. Suddenly, the dark sky was pierced by an unexpected trail of light. The strange light approached Dr. Usui rapidly, becoming larger as it came nearer. Dr. Usui began to feel afraid. He was seized by a powerful urge to get up and flee from that strange light, which was approaching and growing so quickly. However, deep inside him, he knew. That was it. That was no doubt the sign he had been awaiting for so many years. He knew that after so much searching, and for so long, he could not give in now. With a prodigious mental effort, he forced himself to stay put, come what may.

At the very instant his heart made the decision, the tremendous light reached him and struck him hard in the middle of the forehead. Dr. Usui thought that he had died. Millions of bubbles in every color of the rainbow danced in front of his eyes, and then suddenly changed into bubbles of shining white light, each bubble containing a three-dimensional Sanskrit character, drawn in gold. One after the other they appeared in front of his eyes, for just enough time for him to internalize them and engrave them in his memory.

When he felt that the wonderful inspiration of the force had been completed, Dr. Usui was filled with gratitude and joy. He opened his eyes. To his surprise, the sun was already high in the heavens, and a new day of light stretched out before him. Very excited, eager, and happy, he began to run down the mountain slopes. To his great surprise, after 21 days of fasting and endless walking, he felt so strong, so full of life! That was a miracle in itself. He ran, filled with enthusiasm, anticipating how he would tell his friend, the abbot, about the incredible process he had undergone. In his haste, he suddenly bumped into a stone and stubbed his toe badly. Instinctively, in a wave of pain, he stooped to grasp his toe. To his tremendous surprise, a few seconds later, the bleeding stopped, and the pain ceased entirely! His toe had healed completely in a few seconds.

Dr. Usui continued on his way. He reached a roadside inn, and went in for breakfast. The innkeeper noticed his monk's vestments, and understood from the appearance of his face and body that the man opposite him had just undergone a long and difficult fast. He begged him not to eat a full breakfast, and offered him special food, lean and suitable for consumption after such a long fast. It is well known that overeating after a long fast is extremely dangerous. But Dr. Usui did not heed the innkeeper's pleas. He ate his breakfast to the last crumb, and to the innkeeper's amazement, nothing untoward happened to him!

Dr. Usui looked at the innkeeper's granddaughter, who had served him his breakfast. Her jaw was swollen; she had been suffering from terrible toothache for several days. Her grandfather, the innkeeper, was too poor to take her to a dentist in Kyoto, so when Dr. Usui offered to try and heal the girl, he was overcome with gratitude and filled with hope. Dr. Usui placed his hands on the sides of the girl's face. Within a short time, the pain began to recede, and the swelling went down considerably, much to the surprise of the onlookers.

That was not the end of the miracles for the day, however. When Dr. Usui reached the Zen monastery, he found his friend, the abbot, suffering from the pain of a severe attack of rheumatism. While he was telling the abbot about the wonders he had seen on his journey, and about the extraordinary things he had experienced, he placed his hands on the painful areas of the abbot's body. The pain diminished, became progressively weaker, and finally ceased altogether. The abbot was dumbfounded. The energetic Dr. Usui who had followed his heart and his spirit in a search for the wondrous healing powers of Buddha and Jesus, had indeed found the answer.

Now Dr. Usui asked the wise old abbot for his advice about what to do with the wonderful healing powers he had been granted. Again, the abbot encouraged him to meditate in order to receive the answer. After a period of meditation, contemplation, and discussion, he reached the conclusion that he should go out and work with his new-found powers in the beggars' quarter of Kyoto, in the hopes of helping and treating the beggars so that they could receive a new name, as was the custom, become "regular" people again, and integrate into society.

As soon as he arrived in the beggars' quarter, Dr. Usui got down to work. He treated and healed young and old, men, women and children among the wretched beggars. The results were fantastic. Many of the beggars, who were suffering from a wide range of diseases as a result of their way of life, ghastly sanitary conditions, and various accidents, were cured of their ailments. Many of them were cured completely.

Dr. Usui continued his sacred mission for seven years. However, to his great amazement, he began to notice familiar faces. People who had been cured by him were coming back for help; they were sick with strange new diseases, and their lives had not been rehabilitated. One of the beggars, a young man, seemed especially familiar to Dr. Usui. During one of his visits, Dr. Usui said, "You look familiar to me. Haven't I seen you before?" "Of course!" answered the young man. "I am one of the first people who came to you. You cured me, I got a new name, I started a new life. I found work. I even got married. But to tell you the truth, all that involved too much responsibility. It was much easier and simpler to be a beggar..."

Dr. Usui soon discovered many similar cases, and realized that he had missed something. His despair was overwhelming. "Where did I go wrong?" he asked himself in agony. However, he soon understood that with all the will in the world, and his amazing healing abilities, he had not succeeded in teaching these people two crucially important things: responsibility and gratitude. He understood that healing the soul and the spirit were just as important as healing the body. By giving the beggars Reiki without asking anything in return, without healing their souls and spirits, he had simply nurtured the beggar inside them. Now he understood the importance of giving energy, and receiving energy in return for the giving. He concluded that these people had to give something in return for the energy, for the healing they had received, and they had to take personal responsibility for the healing process they were undergoing. That is the reason why Dr. Usui decided that there must be a payment for Reiki: as a sign of taking personal responsibility for the treatment, and a sign of the genuine will to be healed and to rehabilitate oneself.

Dr. Usui gradually devised the five famous Reiki principles. He quit the beggars' quarter, and began to disseminate his theory all over Japan. At the same time, he began to understand with crystal clarity the meaning of the symbols he had received on the mountain, and began to use them in order to train people in the art of Reiki, so that they would accept personal responsibility for their self-healing process and for their physical, mental, and spiritual health. Now he started to instruct and initiate additional teachers. When he neared his death, Dr. Usui initiated one of his most loyal pupils, Dr. Chujiro Hayashi, and transferred the responsibility for continuing his path to him. Dr. Hayashi accepted the responsibility for transmitting and disseminating Reiki, and established the first Reiki clinic in Tokyo.

The next great Reiki teacher became acquainted with Reiki via her personal pain and suffering. In 1935, Hawayo Takata, a young Japanese-American woman, came into the clinic. She was weak and suffering from a large number of organic disturbances, and her face displayed the symptoms of severe depression, as a result of the death of her husband several years previously. Her body was debilitated from grief. Mrs. Takata was about to undergo a high-risk operation in Japan. One night, she heard the voice of her deceased husband imploring her not to have the operation. After she explained to her doctor that she had no intention of undergoing the operation, he realized that she was absolutely adamant, and could not be persuaded otherwise. He suggested that she go to the Reiki clinic, which Dr. Hayashi was running at the time. Mrs. Takata took his advice, and began to undergo Reiki treatment. To her amazement, there was an enormous improvement in her condition – both physical and emotional – and she was eventually cured of her ailments, all the while regaining her strength and *joie de vivre*. She was astounded at Reiki's healing power. She did not require better proof than that of its marvelous power: her health was completely restored, and she had gotten out of the painful cycle of disease and severe depression following the death of her husband.

Until that time, Reiki had been considered the preserve of men only. However, a woman of Mrs. Takata's strength and determination would not let an obstacle like that prevent her from learning the secrets of the healing profession that had saved her life. Until now, Reiki had transcended continents, religions, and languages, and had been acquired as a result of a persistent search, without favoring one belief over any other. Now it would also become a symbol of the equality between the sexes! Mrs. Takata received Reiki I initiation and training, followed soon after by Reiki II initiation and training. She returned to the United States, bringing with her tidings of the new healing.

Some time after she began her healing work in the United States, Dr. Hayashi and his daughter came to visit her. During the visit, Mrs. Takata was initiated as a "Reiki Master," and Dr. Hayashi and his daughter returned to Japan, secure in the knowledge that the work was being performed superbly by a faithful envoy in the United States. As a result of his extraordinarily honed senses, Dr. Hayashi, upon his return to Japan, sensed the approaching war, which would create a deep chasm between Japan and the United States. With his sharp senses, he also understood what the consequences of this terrible war would be. Mrs. Takata, whose senses picked up his concern, went to Japan, where Dr. Hayashi told her of his fears. He felt that he had completed his mission here, and had decided to go on a long journey to the world beyond. In the presence of close friends, clothed in the appropriate ceremonial robes, Dr. Hayashi left his body in a fully conscious manner. Mrs. Takata remained in Japan for some time in order to assist with the funeral arrangements, and from there went on to Hawaii in order to avoid the American-Japanese conflict of World War II.

After the war, Mrs. Takata returned to the United States, where she continued to disseminate Reiki, train many people, and heal many others. During the seventies, Mrs. Takata began to initiate other Reiki Masters. She passed away at the end of 1980, leaving many followers behind her. Since then, hundreds of Masters have been initiated, and thousands of others have studied Reiki at various levels. The number of people whose lives have been transformed by Reiki, or whose physical health and mental and spiritual equilibrium have been restored by Reiki, is enormous. Dr. Mikao Usui's search for the path of marvelous healing was not futile. Reiki lives and breathes to this very day, providing help, serenity, and health to hundreds of thousands of people worldwide.

Reiki stimulates the life energy inside us. Reiki cannot be "imposed," nor can "too much" Reiki energy be transmitted to anyone, because the marvelous thing about Reiki

> The meaning of the word "Reiki" in Japanese is:
> **Rei** - universal energy; **ki** - life energy, which links body, mind, and spirit.

energy is that it reaches the recipient in exactly the amount and manner that he is prepared to receive. In the same way, the power of Reiki healing is manifested. The more a person opens himself up to the wonderful energy, the greater the changes that will occur in his life. Of course, when we receive the gift of Reiki by means of initiation with a Master, the changes that are likely to occur in our lives are far-reaching.

Most of the problems that beset a person, as well as his motives in this world, are the result of "separation." Separation begins between the person and himself, and at the same time, between him and his God. When a person is not at one with himself, he is unable to feel the sensation of marvelous oneness with other people, and then it is possible to see all the regrettable manifestations of separation. People ask themselves, "Who am I really?", and have difficulty expressing – sometimes even acknowledging – their true feelings, sensations, motives, and desires. They vacillate between wishes and hidden passions on the one hand and self-criticism and guilt feelings on the other, find it difficult to accept themselves, and for this reason, have a hard time accepting those around them, and what is happening in their world.

The feeling of oneness, which a person who has undergone Reiki initiation is likely to experience, is stunning in its power and in its ability to change all one's patterns of life and thought, opening a new path to self-knowledge. Sometimes, during Reiki treatment, the practitioner and the recipient feel that they are one. The energy that flows between them unites them. This feeling of oneness is unique and extraordinary, and will probably cause the person to ask himself many existential questions that he was previously afraid to ask, repressing and concealing them instead.

When receiving Reiki, many physical and mental blockages may appear and be released. People will probably remember things and see scenes from their past, which provide certain answers pertaining to difficulties and hardships in the present. They may feel "strange" sensations, a sudden emotional openness, and sometimes even a flood of emotions that had been repressed for so long. But there is no need to worry. As we mentioned before, the recipient allows the energy to reach only the places whose release he can endure. Reiki cannot do any harm. The burst of emotion that he may experience is exactly what he wished for, and what he needs at this particular period of his life. Although the first encounter may be a little bit "alarming," there is never any danger in it.

From his childhood, Master Naharo, who is considered to be one of the great Reiki Masters of our time, recognized the need to disseminate the art of Reiki to every person, even if that person is not a "Master" or a professional healer. Over the years, with the help of his numerous pupils (among them, many who went to India from Western countries), he developed courses in which the Reiki principles, the basic hand placements (for self-treatment and treating others), the Reiki symbols, the basic points to which concentrated Reiki is applied in order to treat diseases and certain conditions – points that resemble acupuncture points or Tsubo points – are taught methodically. This book is based on his theory. Finally, upon recognizing the need for Reiki that exists in the modern world – for the individual, for society, and for the entire world – Master Naharo developed *The Complete Reiki Course*, which provides the pupil with the opportunity to undergo self-initiation.

How Does Reiki Work?

On the whole, Reiki energy is purifying, cleansing, obstacle-removing energy.

A wise Reiki pupil compared Reiki energy to an enormous lake of pure, lucid water. When you place a pump in the lake, pump the water, and let it flow, say, into a drainage canal in a field next to your house, the water cleanses, purifies, and eliminates the dirt that has accumulated in the canal. This is not the end of the process, however. The water that flowed into the canal filters into the earth, is thereby cleansed of the dirt it collected, and eventually returns to the lake and merges with the water in the lake.

The process has been completed. The canal has been cleansed and purified... and not a single drop of the water of the lake has been lost.

Let's move from the lake to the reality of our life.

Our energy field, which also includes our physical body, is extremely sensitive to the energy of thoughts and the energy of emotions. When we experience negative feelings or thoughts about ourselves and about the world, or develop negative thought patterns and beliefs that are neither positive nor useful, this is quickly manifested in an overall effect on our energy field, on our emotions, on our health, and on the entire course of our life.

When we experience these non-positive inner states, the natural and correct flow of energy in our body is disrupted, and various energetic, emotional, and physiological blockages occur.

Reiki energy helps open these blockages by flowing through all the blocked places and moving the blocked energy, at the same time cleansing blockages and helping the inner energy flow move in a balanced, healthy, and correct way.

Reiki energy penetrates all the blocked places in both the energetic bodies and the physical body. It fortifies the entire organism, reinforces its vital force and life, and strengthens the body's natural healing and regenerative powers.

Reiki energy strengthens the chakras and the meridians so that the life energy can pass through the body and around our etheric and energetic bodies in a more effective way.

In the case of various diseases, Reiki energy does not simply reinforce the body's natural power to cope with the diseases, but also opens up our mental layer so that we can understand why we were "given" these diseases, and what lesson they can teach us.

Sometimes there are cases in which a person who is undergoing Reiki treatment gains mental, emotional, or spiritual openness, but still does not feel any improvement in his physical condition. This is no coincidence. Since Reiki energy is in fact activated by a higher "intelligence," it reaches the correct areas in which it is needed, whether it is the physical body or the various energetic bodies.

In other words, Reiki energy first flows to the bodies in which the cause of the disease lies, and only afterwards flows to the bodies in which the symptoms of the disease are manifested.

In the same way, the precise amount of Reiki energy that the person is capable of receiving reaches him – whether this is a little or a lot – and treats the layer that is most important to open and balance at that moment. For this reason, there are cases in which physical changes or relief in the physical condition are not immediately visible. This is because in these cases, the Reiki energy must operate first and foremost in other layers – mental, emotional, thought, and spiritual – so that the disease can be cured in such a way that it will not recur simply because the mental, thought, or spiritual reasons for it were not treated.

Many people believe that various holistic or energetic treatments operate on the basis of "the power of belief" or various psychological effects. This is true of many cases in which holistic methods of healing or balances are employed. There is no doubt, however, that Reiki is not one of them.

You do not have to believe in Reiki in order for it to work. It simply does what it has to do whether you believe in it or not.

Reiki also exerts a significant and obvious influence on animals and plants. It is not possible to claim that there is any type of psychological effect on them, since they lack psychological awareness regarding the treatment they are receiving – but they definitely sense it, and sometimes even "ask" for it.

Having said that, in order to feel the clear-cut consequences of Reiki, it is very important that the person want to be cured. In many cases, it is not possible to cure a person who does not want to let go of his disease, no matter how much Reiki energy flows to him. The desire to be cured is also expressed in the changes the person introduces into his lifestyle and patterns of behavior, thought, and inner beliefs, which are almost certainly the initial causes of the disease or problem.

Receiving, studying, or giving Reiki helps the person to cope better and more correctly with these changes.

The Principles of Reiki

As we mentioned before, Reiki is likely to open up a new world of awareness and understanding to the pupil or recipient. The principles of Reiki help the pupil cope with new insights and with the more aware life that derives from them in a better and clearer way. The Reiki principles serve as directions, points of light along the path, directing the person to his appropriate place.

The first principle: Just for today – I will not get angry

Anger, irritation, nervousness. It's so easy to get angry. Sometimes, we do not look into the depths of the things that make us angry. We don't look into the depths of the feeling of anger. The smallest, dumbest things can get us into the bad and dangerous state of anger. Dangerous for us, and dangerous for others. How many times do we vent our anger on another person for some trifling reason, with the seed of the anger planted somewhere deep in our beings, and is whipped out and exploded as a result of some minor, worthless trigger? The extent to which anger hurts us, first of all, and our surroundings, can be seen if only we open our eyes and look. So many people allow their ego, their fear of losing control, to rule their lives, to harm themselves and those around them, and to turn life into a long journey of power struggles, battles, and angers. It sometimes seems as if anger is an infectious disease. It is rare to see smiling faces in the vicinity of an angry person. Everyone is harmed by his wrath to some extent, and some of the victims of his anger take on the anger that is dumped on them and transfer it onward, hurting more and more people. People who allow their egos and their anger to direct their lives move farther and farther away from their "upper I," from their inner truth, which conceals itself in signs of anger. For how is it possible to be angry without completely ignoring our inner guide, the divine seed that is inside us, the pure truth? In order to be angry, to get irritated or to hurt others, we have to ignore them completely, not heed them, move as far away from them as possible. The farther we move away from the divine seed inside us, the more it seems that it is moving farther and farther away from us.

When we permit our ego to lead us, we suffer from futile expectations, desires, and wishes – sometimes to the point of being destructive. People get angry and become enraged because of an affront to their honor or ego. How is it possible to live a harmonious and natural life when the ego and anger control that life? The non-realization of wishes that originate in our ego, and not in our inner truth or guidance, is liable to turn our lives into a series of endless disappointments, sorrow, and angers. Conversely, when we learn to accept things as they are, when they cannot be changed, we gain peace of mind and serenity.

We often get angry because the people around us do not react to our demands and expectations in the way we want. But we have to remember: we are surrounded by people who in fact act as mirror images, or "inverted" mirror images, of ourselves – "The pot calling the kettle black." It is amusing to see just how angry people can get about exactly those characteristics that they themselves have – instead of using the useful "mirror" that they elected to put up opposite them when they created those ties with the people around them. It would be funny, if it weren't so sad, to see how many parents get angry with their children, completely forgetting that they were the ones who served as role-models and helped them become what they are now!

One of the most important spiritual studies is acknowledging that every situation we face is a kind of "lesson" that teaches us something. It is clear that when we react angrily, we do not learn the lesson, but rather repeat the same mistake over and over again.

When we look deeply into our personal lives, we can see how much our beliefs and thoughts shape the reality in which we live. Thoughts of anger, fury, and resentment will ricochet at us like boomerangs, and then we will have to cope with the blow that we basically aimed at ourselves.

Is it possible to say, "I understand the meaning of anger, this non-positive and unwanted energy, and I will never get angry"? It is not easy to commit to that ... but we must remember this principle: Just for today – I will not get angry; I will not get irritable. What for? What's the use of those non-positive emotions? Will anger change anything? Will it repair whatever is broken, will it move the clock back, will it change the situation? No. It can only make things worse. If we remember, just for today, for this moment, right now, not to get angry; not to get irritable; to do what we have to do calmly, to change what can be changed, and to accept what can't – we will already have taken a significant step toward changing our entire way of life. Just for today – not to get angry, and not to get irritable.

The second principle: Just for today – I will not worry

Worry. Such a commonplace concept, so banal. But actually, when we know that our private providence is looking after us, when we have complete faith in ourselves and in God, is there room for worry? When we know that everything has a reason and a purpose in the universe, why must we worry?

Worry about the past, which takes up a lot of time and energy in many people's lives, is completely unnecessary. We did the best we could in those past situations, according to the wisdom, knowledge, and awareness we possessed at the time. We can learn lessons, learn, and become wiser, but why worry? Worry is such a passive emotion. It does not change things – not for the good, in any event. Worries about the past consume a lot of energy and forces that we need in order to get on with our lives here and now. Why torture ourselves with worries about the past? What's the use? Learning and drawing conclusions from the past are not worry, but rather a process of awareness and understanding, while resigning ourselves to what can no longer be changed, and changing what we are able to change – here and now.

Worry about the present is also superfluous and even dangerous. We create our future, and everything that comes to us is part of a plan of prodigious dimensions, in which we star like leading actors, and we have the personal power to change the course of things in the universal plan that has been prepared for us. Everything that happens to us has a reason and a purpose. Many things that happen are often things that we ourselves invited into our reality – frequently by means of our various worries and fears. Our worries and fears are also liable to assume unrealistic proportions when we nurture them and invest energy and strength in them.

Why worry? If we remember, just for today, for the moment, here and now, not to worry, to do what we have to do calmly, to change what can be changed, and to accept what cannot be changed, we will already have taken a significant step toward changing our whole life. Just for today, I will not worry. When we stop worrying, will nothing work out as we wanted? Will our worry about money, the family, the car that has broken down, safeguard our family? Help us increase our monthly income? Repair the car? What is the use of worrying? The dangers in all those non-positive emotions are enormous – physically, mentally, spiritually-energetically, and of course, environmentally. Many people tend to project their worries onto others, infect them with their fears and worries, or inhibit them as a result of their irrational and illogical worries. Why should we scatter our mental diseases and unbalanced states throughout the environment, infecting everything around us? Why must we introduce negative events into our emerging reality – out of concern for the people around us? Therefore, we have to remember: Just for today – not to worry; to live life as it is, without shouldering unnecessary and useless burdens.

The third principle: Just for today – I will earn a living honestly and decently, and I will do my work with integrity.

Honesty and decency do not have many faces – only one single truth, which we know inside ourselves. Nevertheless, internal manipulations are liable to condone things that are not honest or decent. People tend to say to themselves, "What could happen if I cut corners here or there? Nobody would know..." This attitude, however, is one of the sources of many evils in today's society. When a person adopts this approach, how can he believe in his fellow-man's honesty? How can he look at his own truth, or look himself in the eye?

The path to linking up with the "upper I," with self-recognition, passes through basic honesty and decency. Doing our work the best we can, honestly and decently, is one of the ways to link up with our inner truth. When work is done dishonestly, and not wholeheartedly, not out of truth and decency, we do not feel really worthy and deserving of recompense. Deep inside, we know that we did not do perfectly what we ourselves chose to take upon ourselves. How many frustrations, hardships, internal and external conflicts, and arguments with ourselves and with those around us could be avoided if we only did our work – and it makes no difference what kind of work – out of inner decency and honesty? This way is not only more pleasant – it is also easier and simpler.

When we talk about work, we do not only mean work for the sake of earning a living. We also mean inner work, work on ourselves. Here, too, it is very easy to cut corners. But in order to enjoy a harmonious life – both inner and outer – we have to do this work honestly and decently. The aim of this principle is to develop our inner honesty and decency so that they are manifested in every facet of our lives, and make our lives more serene, full, and pleasant. When a person searches for his own truth, he has to search for the truth in everything, in his every deed. It is very easy to say, "Tomorrow I'll start acting honestly and decently in my inner work and my outer work, and with those around me." Not tomorrow, but now, in the present. Therefore, just for today, I will do my work honestly and decently.

The fourth principle: Just for today – I will be grateful. (I will give thanks for the blessings in my life.)

Many people are outraged by this principle. What blessings? Many people are inclined to view their lives as a sequence of things that "have to be done," "have to be overcome": tasks, debts, difficulties that have to be coped with, sorrow, and tribulations. "What is there to be grateful for? What blessings?" they ask, completely forgetting the many tremendous blessings that they have in their lives. Of course, the first and foremost of them is the very fact that they are alive.

It is said that even in the most difficult situation, there are still rays of light to be grateful for. Many people enjoy good health, a family, friends, a roof over their heads, morning sunshine, birds chirping, without noticing that these things are wonderful, and they must rejoice and be thankful for them. Sometimes, their lives pass by without their being grateful for all the wonderful things in them.

When we live our lives acknowledging everything we have been given and are lucky enough to have, and what we hope and believe that we will be given, we attract additional abundance, happiness, prosperity, and joy to ourselves. Life that is lived with gratitude becomes a life that is full of satisfying and joyous reasons to be grateful. Everything we focus on, and provide with the energy of thought and senses, increases. To the same extent, if we focus on lack, sadness, or the "have not" in our lives, those things will increase. And the opposite. When we live according to the principle of "Who is happy? The one who is satisfied with his lot," the lot that we are happy about, the "have" in our lives, upon which we focus and for which we are grateful, will increase. Focusing on lack, deprivation, on what we want (what we lack or the illusion that we are lacking it), is one of the reasons for greed and avarice, which stem from that fear of lack. When we focus on what we have, on the wonderful blessings we are blessed with every moment and every day, not only will we increase the abundance of those blessings, but we will also live in a feeling of constant satisfaction and happiness.

The fifth principle: Just for today – I will show love and respect for every creature and every form of life

By ignoring this principle, ignoring the obvious fact that we – human beings, animals, plants, and nature – are all one and the same, a single living and inseparable tissue, we now live in a world filled with wars, smog, air pollution, a damaged ecological infrastructure that is constantly showing its bruised face in the form of climatic changes and natural disasters, and a sharp drop in the standard of living and health of human beings as a result of their merciless abuse of the environment. If people only observed this principle, so much sorrow and suffering in the world would be spared human beings and animals, not to mention the planet Earth, which is the victim of the whims of people who try with all their might to subjugate nature and control it, instead of living in harmony with it. Every attempt to imagine a world in which its creatures observe this golden principle broadens the heart and fills it with wonderful hopes for peace, brotherhood, and natural unity.

It is very easy to expect the other person to show us love and respect. Many people are inclined to say, "Let others relate to us nicely and welcome us first, then we'll relate to them in the same way." However, we have to learn that every change begins with "I myself," always, and the first organism toward which we have to show love and respect is ourselves. The meaning of the sentence, "Love thy neighbor as thyself," embodies the open secret: only genuine self-love – and this does not mean the illusions of the ego, but rather healthy and normal self-acceptance and self-esteem – will enable us to feel that same esteem, respect, and love for the rest of humanity and the living creatures that surround us.

The perception of the environment, animals, plants, and other people as different and separate from us is the root of the many ills that afflicted society in the past, and still afflict it now. When we understand that we are all dependent on the tight and inseparable connection between ourselves and our environment, we feel a natural and pleasant commitment to show our love and appreciation to the world. This attitude grants us love and appreciation from the world. When we are aware that we are, at our source, energetic beings, as are all the different life forms around us, we understand that barriers of religion, race, sex, or form do not exist at all, but are just an illusion of our human ability to perceive, which we have to cope with. In fact, when we show our love and appreciation toward every living creature and every life form, we ultimately show love and appreciation toward ourselves. The value of this principle is worth more than gold. When we use it on a daily basis to show and feel love and respect toward every living creature and life form, we heal ourselves, those around us, and the world we live in.

The profound understanding of the Reiki principles, assimilating and remembering them in everyday life, will turn the Reiki that we receive or transmit into a way of life, while taking responsibility for our lives, health, and emotions.

UNDERTAKING

I hereby undertake the following:

1. Just for today – I will not get angry.
2. Just for today – I will not worry.
3. Just for today – I will earn a living honestly and decently, and I will do my work with integrity.
4. Just for today – I will be grateful.
5. Just for today – I will show love and respect for every creature and every form of life.

Date: _____   Signature: _____

Treatment with Reiki

The general action of Reiki on body and soul can be summed up in five main effects, which operate in tandem, and allow one another to work synergistically.

(a) First and foremost, Reiki causes a sensation of profound calm. This factor is manifested strongly when practitioners in other fields of treatment by touch, such as massage or reflexology, who have undergone Reiki training, use these methods of treatment and activate Reiki consciously or unconsciously. Reiki is unlimited, and is transmitted during massage, Shiatsu, reflexology, and so on, while inducing a deeper state of calm in the recipient.

(b) The profound calm and the feeling of release and relaxation bring about the second effect, which is the opening of energetic blockages. This effect may be manifested both in body and soul, and sometimes even invokes "forgotten" or repressed feelings, and helps the recipient understand them better.

(c) The release of tension and pressure, and the opening of the physical and emotional blockages brings about the third effect of Reiki, which is the action of detoxifying the body. The release of the blockages affords a more harmonious, healthy, and balanced flow of life energy through the areas that were previously blocked. In this way, Reiki helps balance and increase the body's action of draining and excreting the toxins that accumulate in the tissues, as well as the toxins that are not "physical," that is, the waste products of emotional and mental "pollution."

(d) The fourth effect is preparing the "obstacle-free track" for the transmission of the universal healing energies, which reach the recipient in exactly the required quantity (and in exactly the correct location), and work on the layers that are in need of healing.

(e) After the body purifies itself of the various toxins in it, it has a greater capacity to receive the universal life force energy that comes to it via Reiki, and store it and use it. This leads us to the fifth effect, which is raising and increasing the body's inner healing power by reinforcing the aura and increasing the person's vitality when the universal healing power begins to exert its healing and curing action.

All these effects together cause the person to open up more to the cosmic forces, to become more spiritually refined, and to broaden and deepen his spiritual ability. It must, of course, be remembered that regular Reiki treatments strengthen his body and soul and enable him to feel physically and emotionally balanced.

After this general description of Reiki's action, it must be remembered that Reiki affects everyone differently and individually. The results of the Reiki treatment are actually determined by the needs of the recipient, which are not always obvious and conscious. Among the widespread results are emotional balance, which we spoke about before, release of blockages, including emotional ones, leading to emotional openness, release from stress, the balancing of energies that operate in the recipient's body, increased creativity, a feeling of replenished energy and physical and energetic strengthening, heightened awareness, and, of course, healing and alleviation of the diseases suffered by the recipient.

One of Reiki's most significant qualities, which makes it unique among many other holistic therapies, is the ability to administer Reiki treatment any time, anywhere. It can be administered to a person in order to alleviate a particular pain, such as a headache or a stomach-ache, even in a crowded place such as a restaurant or a pub.

Having said that, there are several important rules that should be strictly observed when we want to administer a complete or optimal treatment.

* It is best if the treatment is administered in a suitably ventilated room, without cigarette smoke or various chemical odors.

* The lighting should be low-key – preferably from a light that can be dimmed, or a candle. An essential oil burner with suitable aromatic oil can be placed in the room (it should be a genuine, pure oil, not a synthetic substitute). It is important to choose a soothing oil such as lavender, frankincense, jasmine, and so on.

* It is possible to play appropriately soft and gentle music, which will help the recipient enter a state of calm and serenity, or will distract him from disturbing thoughts. It is a good idea to check that the music is compatible with the recipient (the same goes for the odor of the essential oil), since there are people who are bothered by these things for various reasons.

* During the treatment, which can be performed when the recipient is sitting, lying down, or even standing up, using certain techniques, you must ensure that the recipient is in a comfortable position. If he needs a pillow while lying down, he should be given a comfortable pillow; sometimes a pillow under the legs is necessary for people who have an abnormally deep curve of the lower spine (lordosis).

* An extremely important factor to take note of is that the recipient must under no circumstances cross his arms or legs, so as not to cause blockages in the flow of energy. For that matter, the practitioner must also ensure that he himself does not cross his arms or his legs, or have one leg resting on the other.

As we said before, Reiki can be administered in places where it is seemingly impossible to administer treatment, such as crowded places, or on a bus or a train, but the rule of not crossing arms or legs can and must be applied everywhere.

Reiki treatment generally is administered from the top down. Even when we give a "quick treatment" in order to relieve some kind of pain, we observe this rule, but we can concentrate only or mainly on the painful areas, or on the places in which we see a particular imbalance. (Then, too, we first treat the higher area, nearer the head, and then the lower areas.)

How is a Reiki Treatment Performed?

Reiki seems much more mysterious when spoken about than when actually seen. Although, to a certain extent, a first-level Reiki treatment involves intimate touch between healer and patient, it is advisable that every person who intends to study Reiki observe an actual treatment before beginning his studies.

At this point, we will attempt to describe all the stages of a treatment involving touch – first-level Reiki – given by a healer to a patient.

The patient, a man of about 40 years old, enters a small room in which the healer is already waiting. She is a woman of about 50 years old, with graying hair and shining eyes, wearing a colorful cotton dress and no shoes. He is wearing ordinary, loose-fitting clothes. The healer asks him to remove his shoes and leave them outside the room. He does so, and reenters in his stockinged feet.

Meanwhile, the healer has lit a candle under a small dish containing essential oil, spreading a pleasant aroma throughout the small room. Soft music is playing on a tape recorder sitting on the floor. There is no electric light source and the room is illuminated by daylight coming through a wide window veiled by a semi-transparent curtain. The healer receives him and briefly explains the essence of Reiki. This pleasant conversation lasts a few minutes. Next they move on to the treatment itself.

The healer asks the man to climb on to a high, narrow treatment table covered with a white sheet. The table is standing in the center of the room so that the healer has access to the patient from both sides. The man lies down on his back, as the healer instructs him to, with his legs slightly apart and his arms resting at his side. She places a small pillow under his neck and covers his body loosely with a white cotton sheet.

[The small pillow under the nape of his neck helps open the upper chakras. The sheet covering him is effective in three ways: First, during the Reiki treatment, a treatment filled with emotional responses, the patient may perspire, shiver with cold or feel waves of heat (and at times, all of the above, intermittently), and the sheet helps balance him physically. Second, the sheet affords the patient, who is often in an awkward situation in presence of the healer, a feeling of safety. Third, the sheet generally prevents any sort of contact that could be conceived as sexual – absolutely forbidden between healer and patient; since Reiki requires contact between the healer's hands and the patient's body, this danger exists.]

After the patient has relaxed on the table, the healer goes to a small basin and washes her hands under running water and dries them on a small white towel. Remember that the palms of the hands are the most important tool in first-level Reiki and must therefore be kept clean and in working order.

The healer approaches and stands at the head of the table, behind the patient's head. She places her palms on the patient's head, so that his eyes are covered; her fingers are near his mouth and the heel of her hands are resting on his forehead. Almost unconsciously, the healer's breathing and the breathing of the patient reach a similar rhythm. When this rhythm is achieved, the practical stage of the Reiki treatment may begin. The patient will generally feel a sense of warmth while the healer feels tingling in her palms.

The healer holds her hands still for a few minutes with her eyes partially closed. At a certain point, she begins to move her hands downwards alongside the patient's head, chin, throat and shoulders. The movements develop into small circles, the right hand moving clockwise and the left moving counter-clockwise. (However, there are healers who prefer to forgo the circular movements; this does not detract from the quality of the treatment.) Every now and then, the movement ceases and the healer holds her hands over a certain spot for a few minutes. The patient trembles occasionally, but the overall feeling is one of sleepiness.

At this point, the healer moves to one side of the table (it does not matter which side) and continues gently touching the surface of the patient's body with circular motions, until she reaches his feet. When she does so, about half an hour will have elapsed since he entered the room.

(It is important to note that the healer herself determines the speed at which she moves her hands, according to an inner sense that develops over time and with experience. Let the hands move when they want to! Do not construct a solid, precise, schematic plan for a Reiki treatment.)

Now, the healer supports the patient, helping him roll over on to his left side, with his legs slightly bent, as if assuming the fetal position. The healer remains behind him and begins the treatment again, from the head (above the right ear), along the entire right side, down to the right foot. Having completed the treatment, she helps the patient roll on to his right side, moves behind his back, and performs the treatment on his left side, from head to foot. By now, about an hour will have passed.

Now the patient lies on his stomach. He appears sleepy but his body still trembles occasionally. The healer is standing on his right side and is performing Reiki from the head downwards. The main area she is treating now is the spinal cord, along its length and down both sides of it. Her movements are long, similar to those of massage, and not the circular movements she used before.

When the healer completes the entire treatment – about an hour and a half – the patient feels sleepy (and may even fall asleep). In many cases, the sheet is wet with perspiration.

The healer, despite her exhaustion, slowly helps the patient into a sitting position and brings him a glass of water. When he gets off the table, she supports him. (Sometimes, the patient feels the need to sit for a few moments following a treatment, mainly to balance his blood pressure. It is therefore advisable to have a mat or a small carpet in the room, and to teach the patient to sit cross-legged on the rug).

The healer accompanies the patient out of the room. If payment is required, this is done outside the treatment room.

This description is, of course, a general outline of a Reiki treatment.

Presently, we will describe certain situations or phenomena which occur during Reiki treatments, and which will eventually be experienced by every healer. First, however, we must clarify one point.

Remember that Reiki is not harmful. Hence, during a prolonged Reiki treatment, nothing harmful can possibly happen! Even if seemingly alarming symptoms appear, such as perspiration or trembling, they will not do any harm. Therefore, a Reiki treatment must be thorough and ongoing in order for it to afford the patient the best possible results.

Now we will examine different situations and treatments that might come up during a Reiki session.

Weeping

A phenomenon that often embarrasses the healer is deep, heartfelt weeping. It bursts forth suddenly and surprisingly when the healer touches a certain point on the patient's body (mainly around the heart chakra).

It appears as if the patient is crying for no reason at all, but the patient actually has no control over it. This crying must be seen as a channel for purification and cleansing which removes a great blockage from the energy channels. Occasionally, it is accompanied by tears, "which purify the paths of vision," or wailing and groaning, which cleanse phlegm passages.

There is no reason to terminate the treatment if the patient starts crying. The healer must stop moving his hands at the point that has provoked the crying (known as the crying trigger, in professional literature), and wait until the crisis passes.

Loss of Bladder Control

Another well-known phenomenon, and even more embarrassing, is the patient's loss of bladder control (particularly with women). Urine leaks on to the sheet or on to the floor, sometimes even forming a small puddle, and there can be a noisy passing of gas. This phenomenon may occur when the healer's hands are on any part of the patient's body, but mainly when the patient is lying on his side. There is no reason to stop the treatment, except in extreme cases of urine leakage. One must remember that the situation is unpleasant for both the patient and the healer, but it does cease after several treatments (and if it recurs, it must be considered a health/physical problem to be dealt with by a physician).

Heat Waves, Cold Waves, Goose Bumps, Trembling and Tingling

Many phenomena are expressed on the patient's skin: fluctuations in body temperature cause sensations of heat and cold and changes on the surface of the skin. These are natural occurrences which show that the treatment is going well and that the Reiki process has actually begun. Usually, these phenomena disappear after about half an hour. If they continue until the end of the treatment, it indicates that the patient is in a bad way, and a schedule of daily treatments must be planned for the next two weeks.

Bodily Tension

Most healers are aware of the changes in bodily tension. First, the body of the patient becomes rigid and tense, and later the tension disappears and the muscles relax. This is a natural state.

However, the body may be relaxed at the beginning of the treatment, and signs of tension – rigid muscles, for example – appear during the treatment. If these signs do not disappear by the end of the treatment, it indicates that there is a problem the Reiki healer has not located.

In cases such as these, the patient should take a hot bath or have a relaxing massage prior to the next treatment.

Changes in the Breathing Rhythm. Wheezing

We must differentiate between these two similar phenomena. A change in the breathing rhythm is a normal and acceptable occurrence during a Reiki treatment. Usually, breathing changes according to the breathing of the healer, with the patient breathing deeply and steadily. However, occasionally wheezing is heard, and it does not cease within a few seconds.

In cases such as this, the patient must be turned over on his right side and treated until the wheezing ceases.

Asthma Attacks

People suffering from asthma and similar diseases may exhibit signs of asthma attacks during a Reiki treatment session. In such a case, the treatment must cease. Treatments may only continue only after the patient has been treated medically – and not the same day.

Rebirth

On occasion, Reiki leads to a phenomenon similar to that known to occur during the experience of rebirth. The individual feels as if he has been reborn, and display signs of "babiness." Many Reiki healers also serve as rebirth instructors, since the two methods are so similar.

Reincarnation

Reiki often leads to a "path" of reincarnation, and both the patient and healer sense past lives.

Involuntary Meditation

Reiki leads to situations similar to total meditation. The main phenomena are flashing lights in front of the patient's eyes, colored lights resembling fireworks, visions, and a sense of "the opening of the chakras." These occurrences are not at all negative.

Changes in Blood Pressure

Reiki may cause changes in the patient's blood pressure. Usually, it is regulating – high blood pressure is lowered and low blood pressure is raised – but one must remember that extreme changes in blood pressure or extreme levels of blood pressure (high or low) require medical attention.

Blurred Vision

Often the patient senses that his vision is blurred following a Reiki treatment. This condition passes about an hour after the end of the treatment.

Side Effects Following Treatment

Treatment is frequently followed by side effects. These must be monitored, and if they do not disappear after three days, the patient should seek medical advice. Amongst the side effects are:

- Nausea, biliousness, stomach-aches.
- Headaches and migraines.
- Muscular weakness.
- Increased perspiration, sometimes accompanied by a strong body odor.
- Dryness of the mouth.
- Frequent urination.
- Cloudy urine.
- Diarrhea.
- An increase of body temperature by up to one degree.
- Feelings of depression or sadness.

These side effects do not necessarily appear, but when they do – one or more of them – they appear in moderation.

If one of these side effects appears in an extreme form, medical treatment should be considered. The same goes for a symptom (however slight) that does not disappear after three days.

In conclusion, the Reiki healer must prepare a treatment plan for each patient. Usually, the appropriate treatment takes place once every two days over the course of two weeks, and later, one or two treatments each week. It is desirable that the healer prepare the plan at the end of the first meeting and inform the patient of it.

[This chapter is taken from the book by one of Master Naharo's first pupils, Bill Waites, who underwent thousands of Reiki treatments. He wrote the book with Master Naharo, and we thank him.
Bill Waites and Master Naharo, *Reiki – A Practical Guide* (Astrolog, 1998). This book has been translated into several languages.]

Reiki's Influence on Our Quality of Life

One of the most dangerous enemies of a healthy, serene, and balanced life is stress, pressure, or tension. In modern, fast-moving, materialistic, and achievement-oriented society, the daily pressures that we have to cope with are extremely heavy, and we can easily find ourselves in situations of stress or tension at work, on the highway, at home – in fact, almost anywhere.

To all intents and purposes, stress or tension is a physical phenomenon. The emotional process that causes stress activates physical mechanisms. Finding ourselves constantly in situations of pressure and tension exhausts the body as a result of the repeated and persistent activation of these mechanisms, which, from an evolutionary point of view, were meant to serve us in life-threatening situations of stress or tension, so as to make our attack or escape action more effective. Today, however, they are activated over and over again in many people during the course of the entire day. Situations such as falling behind schedule at work, family disputes, study pressures, and excessive demands from children, as well as a lack of consideration for our feelings or emotions, driving along the highway, financial pressures, and so on – all these cause tension, and gradually undermine all the body's systems.

Being in a constant state of stress is liable to exhaust people mentally and physically, and to expose and create various diseases. Reiki, administered regularly, exerts an enormous influence on reducing the stress from which modern man suffers so constantly. Lowering the level of stress is a continuous function of transmitting Reiki energy, and its major significance, besides the immediate sensation that is experienced when receiving Reiki, is the change in perception that frequently occurs in people who are treated with Reiki on a regular basis. Getting into a stressful state is a very subjective matter. Certain people are easily stressed out by things that appear "trivial" to others, while other people have a calmer and more easy-going – and therefore healthier – nature. The wonderful thing about Reiki is that it helps people get things into proportion, so that the pressure that is exerted on them decreases as a result of their inner perception and the change in their outlook on life. Reducing stress and pressure helps people in every aspect of life, strengthens them physically and mentally, and helps them maintain a healthy body and a stress-free mind.

Another area in which it is possible to see the influence of ongoing Reiki treatment is that of emotional balance. Similar to the situations of stress that we experience every day, there are also many emotional roller-coasters from which many people suffer constantly. Mood swings, ups and downs, feelings that are not harmonious, and many emotional states that persistently tax our nervous system, debilitate the immune system, harm the body as well as the thought and emotional layers, and sometimes cause people to become obsessed with negative emotions and thoughts, as a result of which a gloomy, sad, and joyless picture of the world and of reality is created to a greater or lesser extent. It is wonderful to see how effective receiving Reiki regularly is in helping to balance these emotional roller-coasters, and the way in which we interpret, accept, and work through various emotional states. States that previously would have inspired anger, sadness, an emotional outburst, sorrow or irritation in a particular person are now taken on board and interpreted in a far calmer and more relaxed manner after regular treatment with Reiki. What happens when all those emotionally unbalanced states calm down? The enormous amount of energy that was invested in coping with those states and with all those emotions that exhausted body and soul now accumulates in marvelous "reserves" of energy that can be channeled along beneficial and useful paths.

Self-Treatment with Reiki

Many Masters not only encourage their pupils to try self-treatment with Reiki, but actually insist that they do so. And rightfully.

Over the years, Master Naharo devised the set of Reiki exercises he taught in such a way that almost every exercise can be self-administered as well as used as a tool for treating others. *The Complete Reiki Course* starts off with self-treatment, and its aim is to show that treating others is a direct offshoot of self-treatment.

In any event, remember the rule, "Do unto others as you would have them do unto you." After trying out self-treatment with Reiki, you will be more aware of Reiki and its energy. It is advisable for every Reiki pupil to undergo self-treatment, both for learning experience and for self-awareness.

Self-treatment is one of the most powerful ways to understand Reiki's tremendous contribution to every aspect of life, and even more than that, to begin to understand what Reiki really is through intuition and feelings.

In order to illustrate this point, we present the story of Jesse, today a Reiki Master who runs workshops for teaching Reiki.

Jesse, 45 years old, lived an ostensibly ordinary life, without getting too involved in "the meaning of life," as he would put it, using a slightly derogatory tone that reflected his attitude toward the various theories pertaining to self-awareness, universal energies, and so on. He was a successful businessman, married, and father of two grown children, and he lived his life according to patterns he had acquired throughout his life – some of them inhibiting and treacherous, of which he was unaware. His life flowed more or less smoothly – until the accident. When he was 40, Jesse was badly injured in a serious automobile accident. He was hospitalized for a long time with a serious spinal injury as well as a head injury that caused him speech and other functional problems. The accident destroyed his world in the blink of an eye. From a strong, authoritative man who was confident that he was in absolute control of his life, he suddenly became a helpless person who was struggling through a difficult period of recuperation.

That wasn't the end of his troubles, however. While he expected full support from his immediate family, it transpired that his wife was unable – and perhaps even unwilling – to deal with the serious repercussions of the accident on their lives. While Jesse was a successful businessman, a strong, impressive man, she stood by him. Now that he was unable to return to work, both because of the physical and verbal injuries, and because of the mental trauma he was forced to cope with, serious cracks began to appear in the couple's relationship. Broken-hearted, Jesse realized that he had given his heart to a women who was unable to stand by him in times of trouble. The sticky divorce added considerably to his difficulties in coping with and adapting to his new situation and the need to virtually start a new life because of his physical limitations.

As a strong and determined man, Jesse succeeded in overcoming, to some extent, most of the difficulties. His physical rehabilitation was quite good, but the scars – both physical and mental – left their mark on him. He became a bitter person, lacking in confidence in life and in the order of the universe, which had been so cruel to him, and restless, intolerant and irascible in the extreme. These traits, of course, made his life even harder, and although he had recovered quite well from the physical point of view, he had a hard time finding a mate and leading a satisfying and enjoyable life.

In addition to the difficulties in finding work in his present state, Jesse suffered from extremely severe back pains that were so powerful that they sometimes neutralized him. He tried all kinds of treatments, from physiotherapy to various surgical procedures. But nothing helped. Ultimately, his physicians gave him to understand that the pains would be a part of his life forever. Jesse was not prepared to accept this, however. While he was suffering from such agonizing pain, his chances of rebuilding his life fully and well, of working in a satisfying job where he could realize his talents, and even of "calming down" a bit, seemed infinitesimal. He refused to resign himself to the facts.

During a sojourn in a special clinic for people who suffered from chronic problems and severe pain, Jesse met a Reiki practitioner. She was a friendly and tolerant person, and managed to see beyond Jesse's irascible, closed, and bitter exterior. When she told him about Reiki, Jessi reacted in a rude and pejorative manner. But when a wave of sharp pain stabbed his back, he quickly agreed to her trying to "demonstrate" some of the advantages of the method she had told him about. After a number of treatments, Jesse felt significant relief. No other treatment he had tried had helped so considerably. He had no choice but to admit that what she had said was true. After several treatments, the practitioner explained that Jesse could use the method to treat himself, without being dependent on another practitioner. Every time he felt pain, he could alleviate it himself, without medication, and without other people.

These things won Jesse's heart. He felt a fierce desire to learn the method himself so that he could treat himself and would not have to be dependent on others, as he had been for such a long time, because of the accident. The idea that he could treat himself, and could bring relief and help to himself, seemed marvelous to him, even though he found it a bit hard to believe. However, the results were so blatant that he decided to try and learn Reiki in order to administer self-treatment.

After doing first-level Reiki (Reiki I), Jesse began to treat himself. The relief he felt was not only physical. The mental changes that he underwent were very significant. He felt that suddenly his thinking had become more flexible, and that he had become more open to listening, understanding, and accepting things that in the past he would have rejected out of hand. He related to people in a gentler and more understanding way, and suddenly his life seemed less black, sad, and difficult. When he began to treat other people, Jesse was already a different person in his perception of the world. He did Reiki II, continued administering treatment, and saw wonderful results. By means of Reiki, Jesse's "weakness," the huge suffering he had known, the pain and the injuries, became the source of his strength and power. Through them, he was able to make contact with people, and to understand them and be empathetic with their pain and feelings. He quickly became a successful and sought-after practitioner, and went on to become a Reiki Master.

When Jesse told me his story while we were sitting in the large institute for the study of Reiki and other healing methods that he managed, it was difficult for me to believe that the self-confident, smiling, serene, and charismatic man opposite me had been a bitter, irritable, hurt person, who felt anger and resentment toward the whole world. He went on to say that today he thinks about how he could have gone on living with the severe pains, but he could not have gone on living "life" in the true sense of the word with his negative and pessimistic attitude. His life is now full of satisfaction and happiness, and the optimistic, compassionate, hopeful, and grateful outlook on life that he embraced enables him to enjoy every new and fascinating day, and remain steadfast in the face of life's vicissitudes.

Having said this, there is one pitfall of which the aware person, learning to treat himself as a way of increasing his personal awareness and his mental and spiritual growth, must beware.

Many methods of self-awareness and self-treatment are occasionally liable to turn into a way of shirking the basic problems that are inherent in a person's life. When a person suffers from a significant lack of balance in his life, or goes through a severe mental and physical crisis, he has to know that the methods of self-treatment, among them Reiki, do not constitute, in most cases, a substitute for professional help. This is true for an acute mental condition, as well as for a poor physical condition, chronic disease, and so on. The person must be aware and honest with himself, and know when to reach out for help. When one's troubles seem too overwhelming and difficult to deal with at a particular moment, it is important to go and seek professional help. The suitable medical, psychological and holistic treatment, in combination with daily Reiki treatment, full body treatment and self-treatment, will constitute a successful whole with greater chances of achieving optimal balance and health.

In the same way, it is important for the person to understand that even if he administers self-treatments of Reiki on a daily basis, but does not make far-reaching, conscious, and serious changes in his way of life, thinking, and beliefs, if he persists in a way of life that is detrimental to him and the environment, the Reiki treatment will be no more than a "symptomatic" treatment. This is also the case when the person wants to improve his physical condition by means of self-treatment with Reiki, but does not pay sufficient attention to the other aspects of physical-mental health: correct nutrition, exercise, abstaining from harmful habits, and so on. A person who treats himself with Reiki, but eats unhealthily, for instance, or obstinately continues to adhere to unwanted characteristics, such as nervousness, sadness, anger, intolerance, and so on, will find that Reiki is ultimately of very little assistance to him.

Despite Reiki's tremendous power and its physical, mental, and spiritual influence, the treatment itself is not enough. The person must make a conscious effort to go deeply into himself, to examine his way of life and his behavior, and try, in a clear and conscious way, to repair what needs fixing, those patterns of thought, belief, and behavior that limit and inhibit him. Frequently, when we meet people who treat themselves and others with Reiki, and we observe their situation and way of life from the side, we feel that they have missed something. Although they are linked up to Reiki energy, we feel that they are lacking a certain "spark" – most likely because they did not undergo the deep and conscious change that is required in order to achieve spiritual and mental development, and true, lasting physical health.

Krona Reiki

After learning many principles and methods of treatment according to "Usui Reiki," it is worthwhile taking a look at one of the most accepted methods of Reiki, "Krona Reiki."

Krona is a Sanskrit word, used in turn in Hinduism, Buddhism, and Zen, meaning "action full of compassion." This compassion means that when a person is enlightened, he sees no difference between people, and his compassion-filled action reaches every person, without discrimination or differentiation, since he sees all human beings as a single whole that includes himself. According to this perception, the very fact of the tremendous desire to relieve the suffering of others, who are not really perceived as "others," but rather as part of the whole, creates two situations: First, the desire and enlightened perception strengthen the desire itself and turn it into a realistic action. Second, by seeing all human beings as one, by a perception of unity, the alleviation of the suffering of one person heals and helps the whole world. It is not an empty metaphor, but an energetic way of relating to the unity of our souls, which are influenced by one another limitlessly.

Krona Reiki has its own abilities, and it is no less powerful and significant than Usui Reiki. Krona Reiki operates simultaneously on the energy bodies, and its practitioners claim that it is more tangible and concrete. Moreover, they say that the energy of Krona Reiki surrounds them, and the recipients feel an additional sensation beyond the feeling of the energy that envelops them – that of beneficial grounding.

People who undergo Krona Reiki initiation experience a connection with their instructors, with their angels, and with their "upper I," as well as the healing presence of beneficent beings.

Similar to the marvelous work of Dr. Usui, who received Reiki and the special knowledge through meditation and spiritual work, so too William Rand, the person who developed Krona Reiki, reached his insights and enlightenment through meditation with Reiki symbols. By means of this meditation, he discovered ways of augmenting the power of the symbols, and of increasing their abilities. By means of this meditation, he himself went through attunement for Krona Reiki, and founded the new order.

Krona, that is, action full of compassion, is the quality of all the light entities that operate around us. They operate regularly, and their blessed light influences every creature. However, not every person has the ability to receive this light. That is, abundance and blessing are affected, but what determines their final and healing effect is each person's individual ability to receive. The people who undergo initiation for Krona Reiki increase their ability to receive those blessed lights enormously – if they use them in order to help and benefit themselves and others, when, of course, according to this perception, they are all one. The uniqueness of this method, therefore, is that by working with it, it exposes us to closer work with the enlightened entities. We may encounter these entities in their ethereal or spiritual form or possibly in human form, if it is necessary to work closely with them. People who are experienced in this type of Reiki relate wonderful things about the sensations that arise while receiving Reiki, and about the amazing results of treatment. However, the best result will be achieved from a merging of Usui Reiki and Krona Reiki. In any event, in order to send long-distance Reiki, the two methods should be combined.

Personally, I (Gail) prefer the traditional Reiki method, especially Master Naharo's version, and I do not use Krona Reiki.

Reiki I Diploma

The Reiki I diploma is hereby awarded to

_____

upon learning and internalizing
the Reiki principles.

  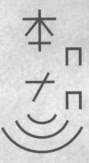

This diploma qualifies _____
to receive the blessing of Reiki and to confer this blessing upon
others by means of thought, in any manner he/she considers correct.

Master Naharo

PART 2
Reiki Exercises

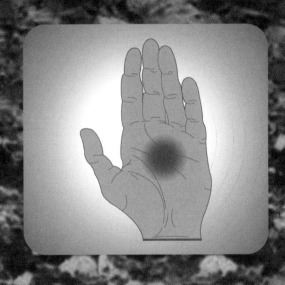

The Main Reiki Symbols

In this chapter, we will discuss the dozen main Reiki symbols, and learn the correct way to sketch them, their uses, and their importance. The twelve symbols are:

1. **Cho-Ko-Rey – power**
2. **Se-He-Key – (emotional) balance**
3. **Hun-Sha-Zi-Shu-Neen – healing (from a distance)**
4. **Di-Ko-Miyo – energy**
5. **Dai-Ku-Miyo (Rama) – powerful energy**
6. **Rakku (Gnossa) – the fire snake**
7. **Rakku-An – the rolling fire**
8. **Saa-Saa (Eah-Vah) – reinforcement**
9. **To-Ho (Shanti) – love**
10. **Zonar – karma**
11. **Har-Te – harmony**
12. **Ha-Loo – truth**

The set of Reiki symbols is an extremely powerful set of tools that grants the user the ability to augment the flow of Reiki in his own body and in other people's bodies, and direct and focus the Reiki energy on places, systems, and certain applications. There are different approaches toward the Reiki symbols, their importance, and the degree of "secrecy" surrounding them.

In traditional Reiki, the symbols were sacred, jealously guarded, and conferred upon the pupil at the end of the initiation stage in an impressive ceremony. The pupil would undertake to keep the symbols a secret and not pass them on to any else (unless it was to a Master who qualified pupils). In some Reiki methods, the symbols were given at the end of Reiki II initiation, and only then did the pupil begin using them. (There are, however, methods of initiation that transfer the symbols to the pupil at the end of Reiki I.)

The question is: What are these mysterious Reiki symbols?

The mysterious Reiki symbols are the symbols that Dr. Usui received when he received the gift of Reiki. The symbols themselves contain the intentions of healing. With their help, it is possible to use additional powers that anyone who has not received Reiki II training and initiation cannot use. Even if someone were to receive drawings of the symbols, there is no way he could use the power that they contain without Reiki II training and initiation. (It should be remembered that this is the opinion of the traditional Reiki Masters.) These three symbols (which are customarily given at the end of Reiki II training) are the expression of Reiki's healing energy. The Reiki II practitioner uses them for self-healing, for healing others, and for sending long-distance Reiki. Working with symbols greatly reinforces the transmission of energy, as well as shortening the treatment time and increasing its power.

Each symbol has a different meaning; they are used for different actions, separately and together, during a Reiki treatment, or for sending long-distance Reiki using various techniques.

In *The Complete Reiki Course*, we adopt a different approach – we present the reader with the 12 central Reiki symbols, reveal the way they are drawn, and provide an explanation of their nature. In our opinion, there is no need for either excessive secrecy or the payment of a special fee in order to receive these symbols.

We must nevertheless remember that the known Reiki symbols, those powerful symbols, will only be useful and effective in the hands of pupils who have undergone the appropriate training in Reiki or have learned the theoretical material from a text such as this book. If you do not know the principles of Reiki, and have not yet assimilated them, knowledge of the symbols will not be of any use to you.

The symbols appear in Japanese-Chinese letters or styles. This is because the Japanese were the ones who revived Reiki in the New Age. However, we must remember that the Reiki symbols are exactly that – symbols – whose power stems not from the fact of being transcribed, but rather from the movement that is performed while drawing them and from the feeling that arises in the person when he draws, looks at or imagines them in his mind's eye (similar to looking at a Mandala).

It is important to remember that we are presenting only 12 of the most common and best-known Reiki symbols. Besides these 12, there are many other symbols that are transmitted by certain Masters to their pupils during initiation and training, such as the symbols of the dragon's Fire, Peace, Midas Star, Trinity, and many others. Most of those symbols can be charged by means of the first Reiki symbol, Cho-Ko-Rey, in order to enhance their action. In addition, every read can "invent" his own Reiki symbols – preferably after a period of work and acquaintance with the Reiki energy – and use them as personal Reiki symbols.

It is important to remember that Reiki symbols have a meaning of their own; it can even be said that they have a "personality" of their own. For this reason, they must be used for the right purposes, and with all due respect. In other words, they must not be used "extravagantly" and lightly, but rather applied appropriately in the right place and at the right time.

Daily meditation using one of the symbols the reader feels right with – a symbol whose meaning you need in order to increase your power to heal and to be of use, and for your spiritual development – is extremely powerful, stimulating, and spiritually elating.

It is important to know each of the Reiki symbols on several planes:

You must know the name, the nickname, and the properties attributed to each symbol.

You must know the shape of the drawing of the symbol, the direction of the drawing in the different segments of the symbol, and the amount of pressure while drawing.

You must know the meditative significance behind every symbol.

In addition, in accordance with the principle of thanksgiving (one of the five Reiki principles), and out of respect and gratitude, it is important to thank every symbol before and after using it. This thanksgiving will reinforce the power of the symbol and make it more effective and powerful when it is used.

The Reiki symbol must be sketched in its correct form, and Reiki healers must remember and assimilate them well, so that they can meditate with them easily and see them in their mind's eye at any time. Beginners are advised to try to draw the Reiki symbols a number of times with a paintbrush for ten minutes every day without looking at the paper on which they are sketching the symbol – at least ten times for each symbol – until they perfect the drawing of the sacred signs. A mistake in drawing the symbol does not cause any damage, since Reiki is the universal energy of love, which only cures and does no harm. Having said that, the incorrect drawing of the symbol can diminish its effectiveness or not produce the desired result (if any). Therefore, it is extremely important to persist in practicing and remembering the symbols until they become part of you and flow naturally during treatment.

Another way to learn the Reiki symbols is by means of drawing them with finger-paints or water colors applied to your finger. After the reader can draw the symbol correctly, he must practice drawing it with his finger (without paint) on his own body or on someone else's body.

Finally, we will stress once more that the symbols will be engraved in the subconscious of every reader, and by visualizing them, he will be able to evoke them and use them at any time.

Now we will present the 12 symbols together with an accurate outline sketch of each one. The link between the various symbols and the hand placements is presented in the chapter dealing with hand placements.

1 Cho-Ko-Rey – Power

The first Reiki symbol is the symbol of power. It is spiral-shaped, and is used for bestowing strength and power, and for reinforcing the self-healing power of the body, soul, and spirit. It strengthens the power of Reiki, and is used to purify rooms, vehicles, and means of transportation in which non-positive energies can be felt, by transmitting a pure white light into these spaces. This symbol also serves as a protection, for charging the other symbols, for purifying food and drink, and for visualizing any part of the body – physical or mental.

The symbol can be outlined clockwise – that is how it relates to heaven, or the "masculine" energy, or anti-clockwise – that is how it relates to earth, or the "feminine" energy. When the two directions are combined, they can be used for charging other symbols, and for sketching the symbol of the "Karia" in the Krona Reiki method.

The symbol is sketched in three stages or "segments" (even though the sketch is in fact performed in one movement). The pressure on the paintbrush increases on the second line.

As we said above, it is possible to focus the symbol on feminine energy (this can only be done by women) or on masculine energy (this can only be done by men). In the event of this focus, the sketch is performed as follows:

For a man, segments 1, 2, 3 as described above, in the same directions, except that now the strong pressure is applied in segment 3 in its entirety.

For a woman – segments 1, 2 as described above, with strong pressure applied on segment 2. At the end of segment 2, the finger or paintbrush is lifted, and segment 3 is sketched anti-clockwise: the finger is lifted, placed on the point marked X, and segment 3 is sketched to point Y.

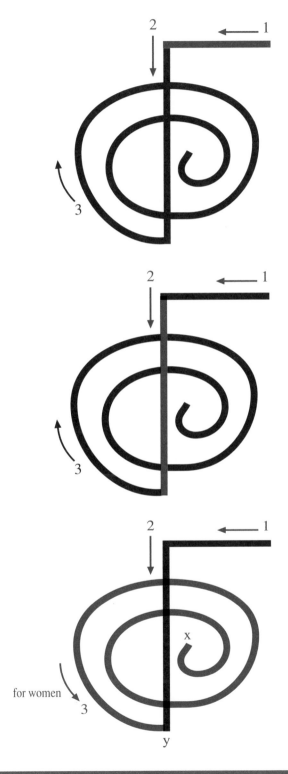

2 Se-He-Key – (emotional) balance

The second symbol is the symbol of thought and feeling, and is extremely significant in the treatment of old, inhibiting patterns of belief, thought, and emotion. It means that God and man are one. It is used for emotional and mental balance, and for creating balance between emotion and reason, and between the two sides of the brain: the right brain, which is responsible for the actions of the left side of the body, and for creative and emotional activities, and the left brain, which is responsible for the actions of the right side of the body, and for logical, verbal, and analytical activities. Balance between the two parts of the brain leads to the attainment of a feeling of serenity, harmony, and inner peace. In principle, Reiki energy reaches every place that needs it. Therefore, when we want to treat the emotional body, we avail ourselves of this symbol.

The use of the symbol for attaining mental balance and treating old, unnecessary, and inhibiting thought patterns soon leads to the attainment of emotional balance and to far-reaching changes in the person's way of life.

In this subject, it is important to point out that the reality that we experience is to a large extent the reflection of our beliefs and thought patterns – some conscious and some unconscious. Many of them stem from childhood, from traumas that originated in events that were awful and traumatic in the eyes of a small child, but not so difficult and frightening in the eyes of an adult. As a result of the accumulation of these traumas, which were repressed in the subconscious, many adults exhibit irrational fears and illogical, inhibiting, and disruptive thought patterns.

Another type of thought and belief pattern comes from the things that were said to the child when he was young, as well as during his adolescence. Because of his unconditional faith in adults, he internalized these declarations as absolute truth. Statements such as "You're a loser," or declarations that were uttered among the adults, such as "All men are the same; they don't care about their wives..." and so on – harsh and limiting declarations – become inhibiting patterns of thought and belief that the adult carries with him, without disagreeing with them or appealing them. In most cases, he is not truly conscious of the root of his inner beliefs. These beliefs will come true and become the reality of his life. The same child who was labeled a "loser" is liable, one way or another, to have this declaration come true in his adult life.

Many people are not aware of these inhibitions. They ask themselves why those same limiting scenarios, such as marital problems, a constant shortage of money, and so on and so forth, keep on occurring in their lives.

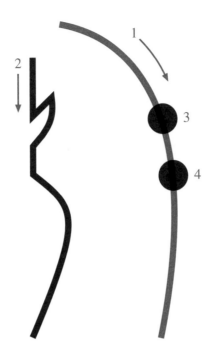

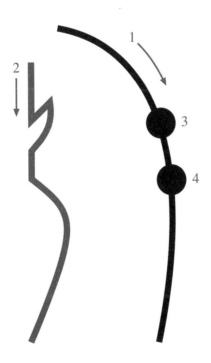

Reiki treatment with this symbol may well raise these thought patterns to the conscious level. Sometimes, a change occurs in the person's thinking without him even being conscious of it. Sometimes, he is struck by the knowledge that he has spent his life dragging inhibiting patterns like these behind him. Sometimes, he will recall experiences in which these thought patterns or various childhood memories were forced on him.

It makes no difference how the inhibiting patterns of thought and belief are changed, but the minute it happens, the person is likely to experience far-reaching changes in his life. Limitations that plagued him for years will suddenly be removed, and he will begin to feel, think, and believe in a different reality – one that is better and more correct for his adult life.

Very frequently, the change in patterns of thought and belief also alters or heals physical problems whose source lies in the direct or indirect after-effects of these thoughts or beliefs, which exert a significant influence on the processes in the body. Many psychosomatic illnesses such as asthma and so on are cured by treating inhibiting patterns of thought and belief.

Besides its use for mental and emotional treatment, the second symbol also serves to improve memory, learning, and understanding, to break bad habits such as smoking, overeating, and so on, to treat unbalanced emotions that disrupt everyday life, to remove negative energies from the chakras, to improve marriage and conjugal life, to soothe the conscious brain and achieve serenity and inner quiet, to cleanse the subconscious of traumas and residual baggage, to treat numerous problems of imbalance in children, and to facilitate the emotional changes and confusion that occur during adolescence.

Another use of this symbol – exceptional among the touch therapies – is in locating mislaid objects and remembering events, people, names, telephone numbers, and so on.

The symbol is sketched in two stages or two separate segments, with two additional strong "touches" or "pressures" with the fingertip or paintbrush. There is great importance to these touches. We must ensure that when we perform them, the paintbrush is held in the right hand (even if the person is left-handed), or that the right index finger is used.

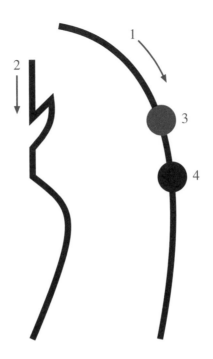

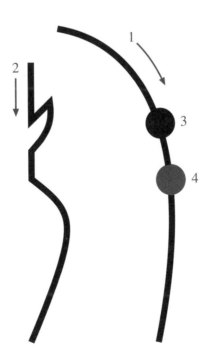

3 Hun-Sha-Zi-Shu-Neen – (long-distance) healing

The name of the third symbol means "The God within me blesses the God within you for bringing healing and enlightenment." This symbol is the most important of the symbols for long-distance Reiki treatment. Because it has no limitations of distance, time, or space, it can be used for changing past traumas (together with the second symbol, for instance), various karmic problems, and so on. It is used for sending Reiki to people and to past and present events, and for constructing a communication bridge between sender and recipient.

It is used for sending Reiki anywhere in the world – to any person, object, event, or situation. It can be sent to future events or situations, such as an important meeting, an exam, and so on, in order for the Reiki energy to be present during the event, influence it in a beneficial way, and help accomplish the objective in a healthy, serene, and optimal manner.

It is very effective when it is sent to a traumatic event in the past, which we want to erase from our present life, together with its influence, as well as to any unpleasant event whose memory and influence we want to erase. Of course, it can be used when we want to administer treatment without physical contact, because it strengthens this kind of treatment wonderfully, in a similar way to its influence on long-distance treatments.

It can be used for treatment when we do not want to place our hands on a person's groin or breasts, when the recipient does not feel comfortable with physical contact for some reason, or is afraid of it, or when, because of a physical condition such as a burn or an infected or open wound, it is impossible or inadvisable to place our hands on the recipient's body.

This is a complex symbol, built of three separate units: past/present/future (apparently) that merge into one dimension.

Past – segments 1 (downward), 2 (from right to left), 3 (the entire angle), 4 (from left to right).

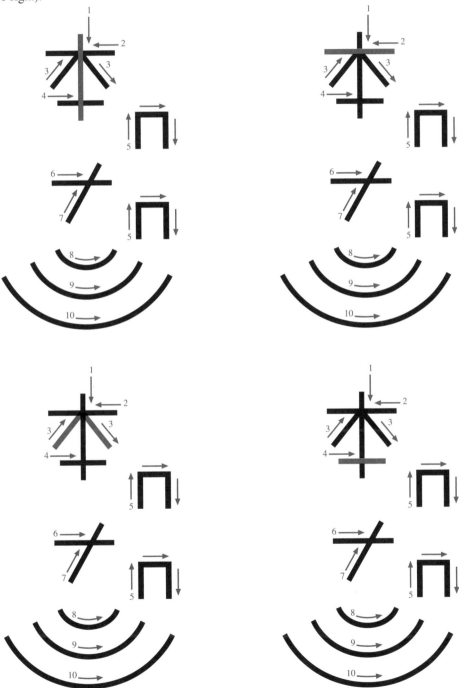

A dividing sketch (5) that is drawn in one movement.

Present – two segments (6, 7) in which strong pressure is exerted.

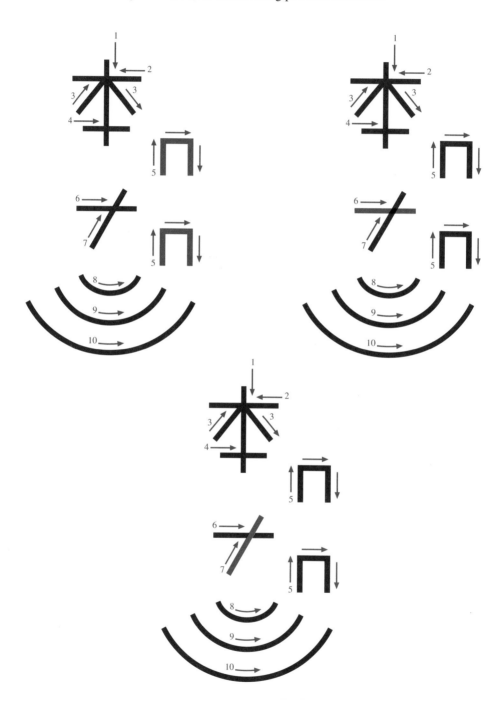

Another dividing sketch (5).
Future – three curved segments.

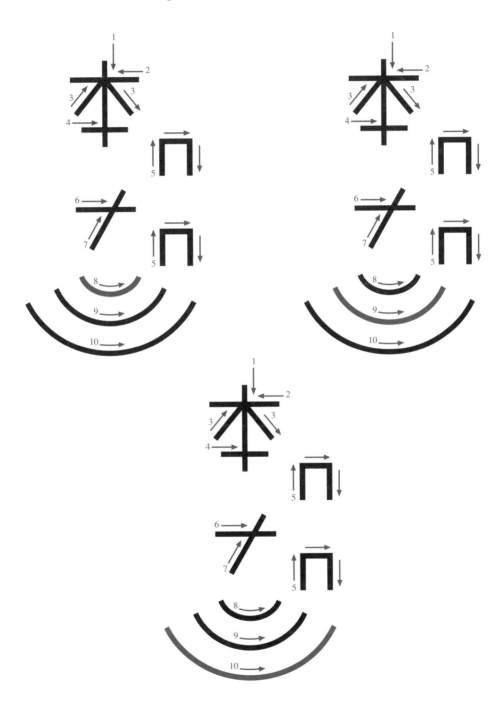

4 Di-Ko-Miyo* – energy

This is Usui's Master symbol. It operates at higher frequencies than the first symbol, Cho-Ko-Rey. When a more effective and speedy result is desired, or when there is a need for substantial or immediate healing, this symbol, in conjunction with the first symbol, Cho-Ko-Rey, has an astoundingly powerful action. When this symbol is used, it enables the energy and the unlimited divine wisdom to manifest themselves on the physical-material plane. It focuses and greatly reinforces the power of Reiki for attaining a stronger and speedier result, and leads to a greater feeling of perfection, unity, and fullness. Its use strengthens and blesses any action.

Since it is a symbol with a karmic action and significance, many Masters recommend that it not be used for regular or general treatments, but only for Reiki initiation by the Master, and for self-reinforcement by means of daily meditation.

This symbol is sketched in six segments, with strong pressure exerted on the horizontal segments. It is important to close the triangles at the base of the symbol well.

---

* As we have mentioned several times, in traditional Reiki, there are degrees of Reiki that are also linked to the symbols. The first three symbols are given to the pupil during Reiki II. Third-degree Reiki (Reiki III) is the degree of Master. After receiving attunement for Reiki III – the degree of Master – these people can help others become transmitters of Reiki themselves. The uniqueness of Reiki Masters, as opposed to masters in other treatment methods, lies in the fact that they are not part of any "superior organization." They are their own masters, and are motivated by the desire to transmit Reiki in the world, and to help many other people by transmitting and teaching it. Some people divide Reiki III into "Master" and "Master Teacher," but the form of Reiki III that is accepted by most Masters is that of "Master and Master Teacher" simultaneously. In the opinion of those who support the traditional approach, Reiki III (including conferring the degree of Master) must be transmitted by direct initiation (by the experienced master). Self-initiation at this level is not possible.

At the level of Master, more symbols are added to Reiki treatment. Some of the symbols are used only by some of the Masters who operate throughout the world today. The most important of these symbols, according to this approach, is the fourth symbol, Di-Ko-Miyo, which is the symbol of the Master. With its help, the Master administers treatment, and also gives initiation and training, so as to qualify new practitioners and initiate them in Reiki.

In this book, we support a different approach. The reader learns the 12 Reiki symbols and uses them for his needs in accordance with his personal development.

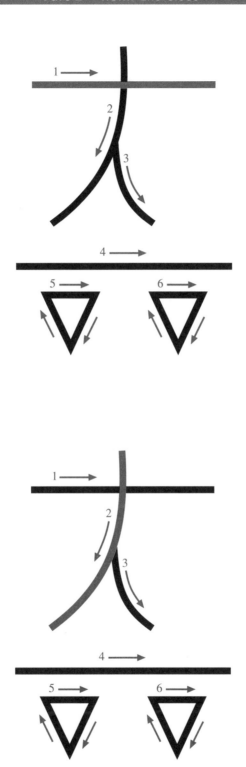

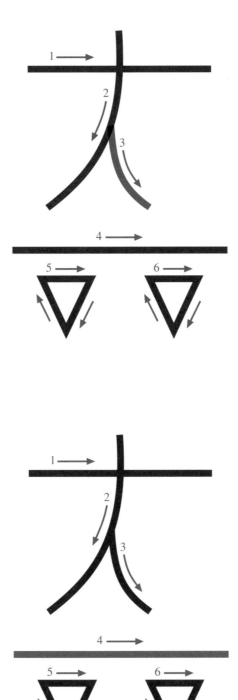

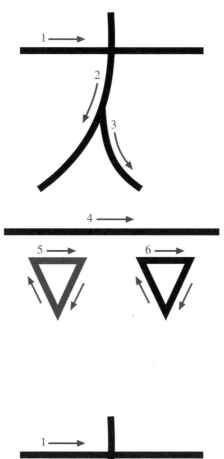

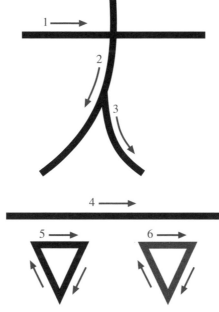

5 Dai-Ku-Myo – powerful energy

This symbol is actually the "double" of the fourth symbol, and is somewhat reminiscent of the first symbol as well. It is also sometimes known by the name Rama. The general use of the symbol resembles that of the fourth symbol, except that this one is considered to be stronger.

In addition, this symbol is used for linking up to the earth and the spirits of heaven. It is used for opening and balancing the lower chakras, for balancing the lower and upper chakras, for cleansing rooms of negative energies, for purifying crystals, for strengthening and reinforcing objectives and the ability to accomplish them. (Of course, it should be used for clean and pure objectives for the benefit of humanity in general. It is not at all desirable, to put it mildly, to use it for objectives that are not pure, or that are unhealthily selfish.) Moreover, the symbol is also used for various grounding purposes as well as protection, such as the protection and grounding of vehicles, against accidents, and safeguarding property and money in business.

The symbol is sketched in two curved segments and with two strong pressures exerted by the left index finger or with a paintbrush held in the left hand.

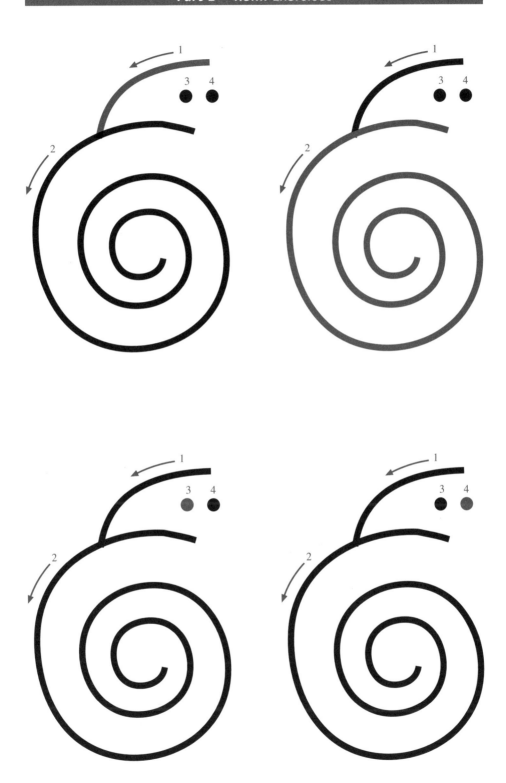

6 Rakku – the snake of fire

The Rakku symbol is sometimes also known as "Gnossa," and is used for joining the person more closely to his "upper I," and for receiving higher awareness and bringing it to the physical body, while creating suitable awareness. It is used before meditation connected to the crown chakra in order to create a link with the "upper I," and in order to reinforce the power of a crystal web and charge it.

The symbol is sketched in two strong lines – a horizontal line and a descending jagged line. Some people recommend that the first segment be sketched with the right hand and the second with the left.

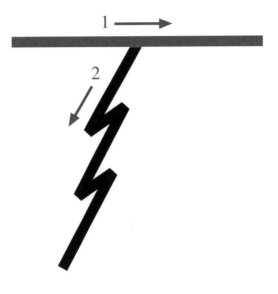

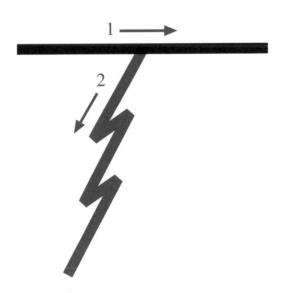

7 Rakku-An – the rolling fire

Rakku-An is in fact the sixth symbol, which is meant to be used by women only. (If this is the case, the use of the Rakku symbol is for men only.) Some of the Masters unite the two symbols, and teach men only to sketch the first shape (6) and women only to sketch the second shape (7).

The symbol is sketched in two strong lines – a horizontal line and a descending "rolling" line. Some people recommend that the first segment be sketched with the right hand and the second with the left.

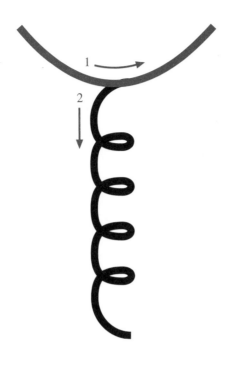

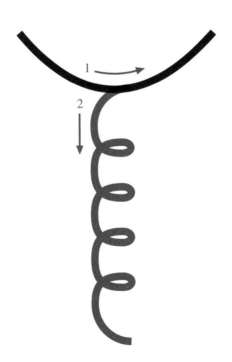

8 Saa-Saa – reinforcement

This symbol is also known by the name of the symbol Eah-Vah (meaning love). This symbol creates our reality as our exclusive reality, without anyone else's influence or projection. It is used for projection onto plants that are in danger of wilting in order to revive them, for turning objectives and projects that are still at the conceptual stage into realities in the physical world, and for realizing aims and ambitions.

This symbol is sketched in four segments, when the first and fourth segments are sketched strongly.

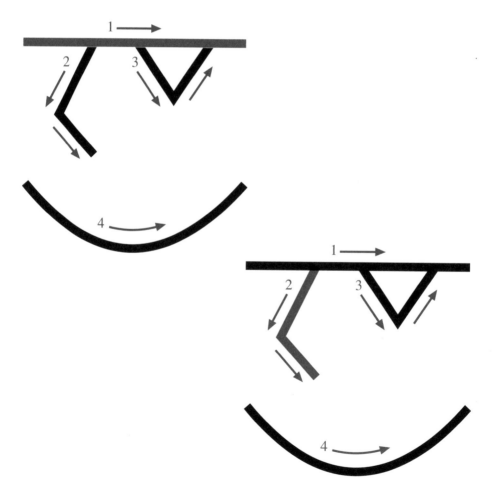

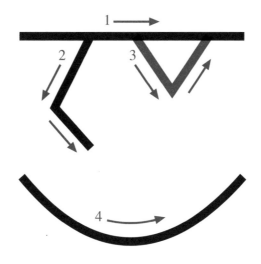

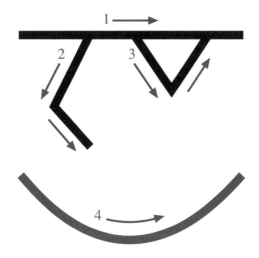

9 To-Ho – love

This symbol is also known as Shanti. The eleventh symbol releases fears and anxieties, nightmares and bad dreams, and affords a harmonious and peaceful life in the present. In this way, it helps create a better, more peaceful, and more harmonious reality. Many people use it in conjunction with the eighth symbol, Saa-Saa (Eah-Vah), for expressing ambitions and desires in the physical world, for their material realization, for healing the past, for opening the third eye, and for cleansing and completing the aura, while reaching a state of calm, peace, and serenity.

This symbol is sketched in three segments, exerting the same amount of pressure as far as possible. There is a difference between the To-Ho symbol as sketched by a man and the same symbol as sketched by a woman. In both cases, segments 1 and 2 are sketched in the identical manner, but the direction of the third segment is different:

For a man, the third segment is sketched clockwise, that is, to the right.

For a woman, the third segment is sketched anti-clockwise, that is, to the left.

You will no doubt notice that the joining of the two segments creates a heart shape, and this is no mere coincidence.

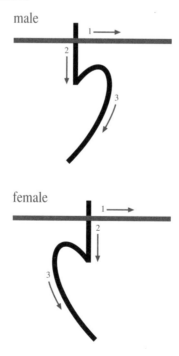

male

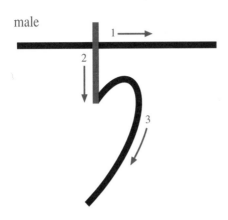

female

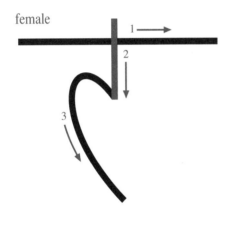

male

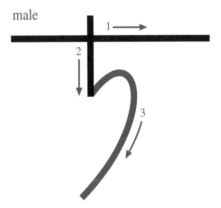

female

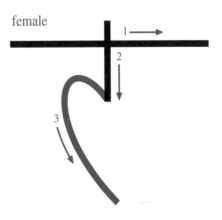

10 Zonar – karma

This symbol is used for treating karmic problems, problems of previous lives, or problems in the present that are influenced by previous lives. It is very effective in treating various emotional problems. It is used for removing traumas from the subconscious, for treating problems that stem from karma or from previous lives, and for treating children and adults who were physically, mentally or sexually abused in childhood.

The sketch of the symbol is complicated, and is performed in five stages:
First stage – upper angle sketched in one continuous movement.
Second stage – upper spiral sketched in one continuous movement, starting exactly at the beginning of the line of the upper angle.

Although we stress the accurate sketching of the symbols, it is important to remember that the main thing is the shape and the flow of the symbol, and not its absolute "accuracy." If your sketch is somewhat different than the exact sketch shown here, don't worry. The important thing is that you feel that **for you** the symbol is correctly sketched.

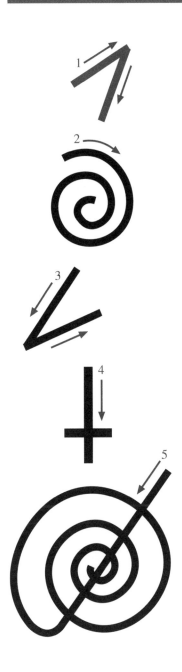

Third stage – lower angle starting exactly at the beginning of the upper spiral, also sketched in one continuous movement.

Fourth stage – a joining line that is sketched in two segments, first the vertical, then the horizontal.

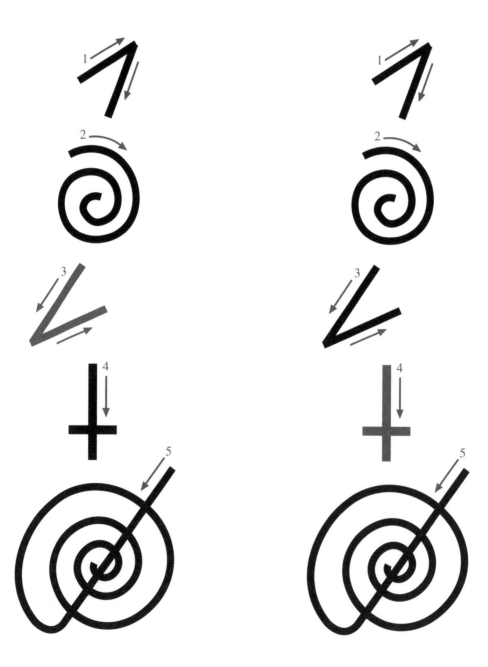

Fifth stage – lower spiral that starts at the end of the straight line (on the right side) and is sketched entirely in one continuous movement, with the inner end point exactly below the end of the vertical line from the segment of the fourth stage.

11 Har-Te – harmony

This symbol, which is pyramid-shaped with a cross in its center, symbolizes love, truth, beauty, harmony, and balance. It is used for treating emotional problems and for any situation or problem concerning the heart – the center of love, receiving, and giving. It is also used in cases of unhealthy relationships, or problems in the relationships between family members, parents and children, siblings, couples, and close friends, and in treating any problem that might arise. It helps develop the Krona – a Sanskrit word that means "an action full of compassion," which symbolizes a profound situation of "Love thy neighbor as thyself" – love and compassion for another person deriving from a feeling of unity and the understanding that we are all one, that another person's pain and suffering are in fact our own pain and suffering. The symbol can be used in order to increase the will and lust for life, and for that reason it is good for use with seriously ill or terminal patients who have lost the will to live, with frail infants whose lives are in danger, and with anorexic people or people whose actions indicate that their innate will to live is defective (people who live in a way that leads to a slow death, a destructive and dangerous lifestyle, and so on). It can be used for rebuilding love and the desire for a normal career and profession, for treating addictions, and for meditation.

People who used it during meditation report that it causes an extremely powerful and arousing experience.

This symbol is sketched in six segments, when segments 1 and 2 are sketched using strong pressure, and the rest of the segments are sketched with lighter pressure. It is important to ensure that all the segments are sketched with absolutely straight lines.

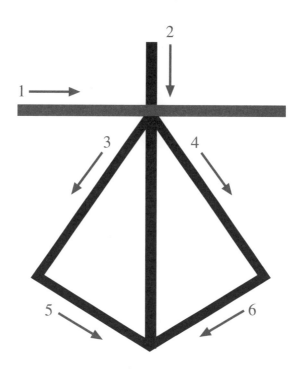

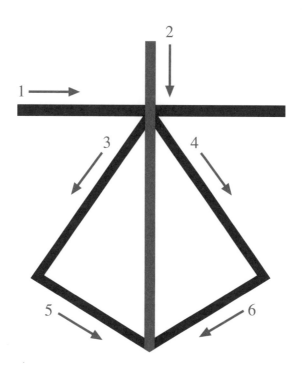

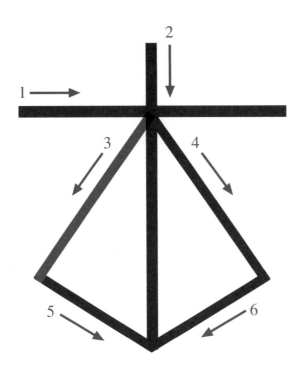

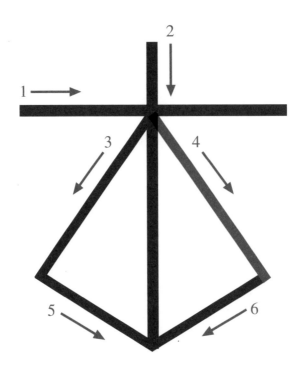

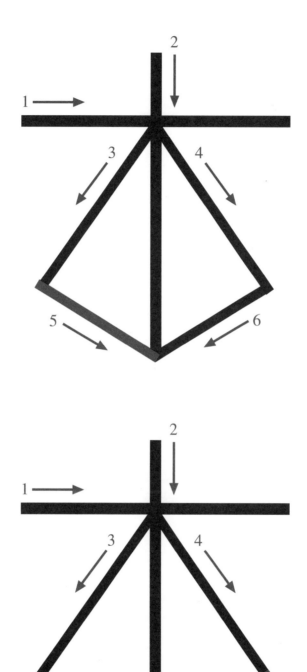

12 Ha-Loo – truth

This symbol constitutes a kind of completion of the tenth symbol, Zonar, enhances its action (and for that reason is stronger), and operates on a higher level. Moreover, this symbol can be a substitute for the eleventh symbol, Har-Te, and reinforce it.

This symbol is used for deep healing and for restoring physical, mental, and spiritual balance, for treating mentally deficient children, for breaking negative mental patterns (even the deepest and strongest ones), for attaining higher awareness, and for treating cases of physical or sexual abuse, rape in the family, battered women, and so on. Moreover, it is used for releasing karma.

The symbol is sketched in seven straight segments (ensure that they are straight) when the horizontal segments (3, 5, and 7) are sketched with stronger pressure. It is important to ensure that the segments are sketched in the order shown in the diagram.

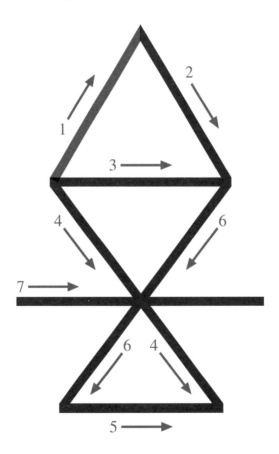

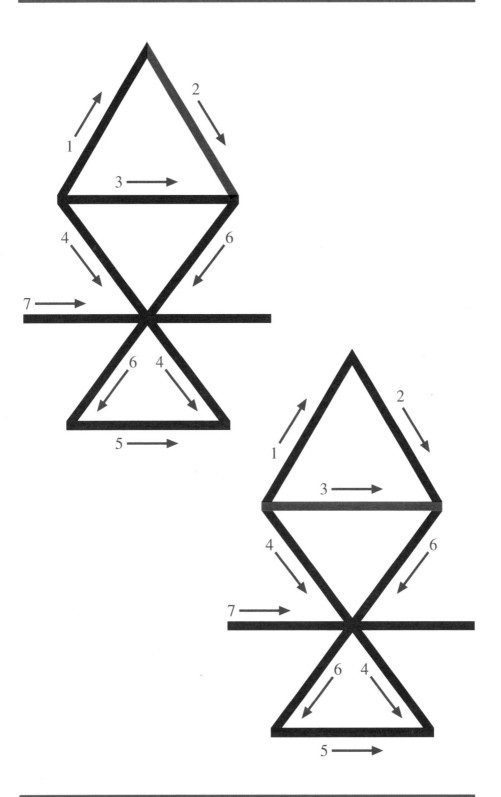

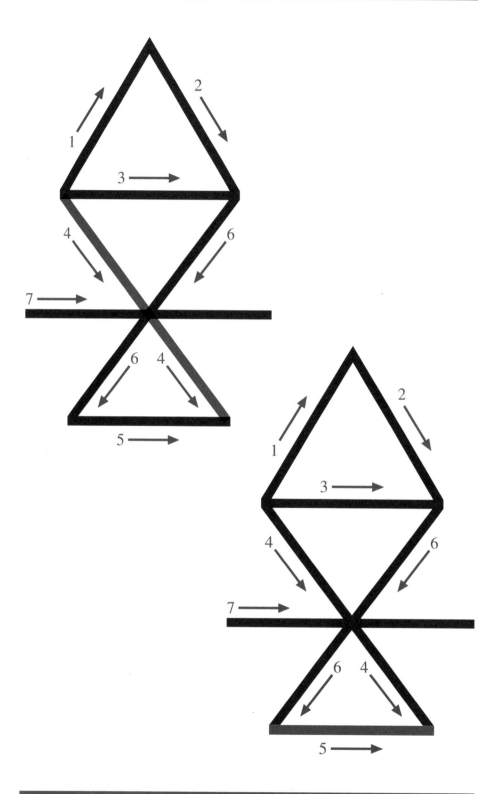

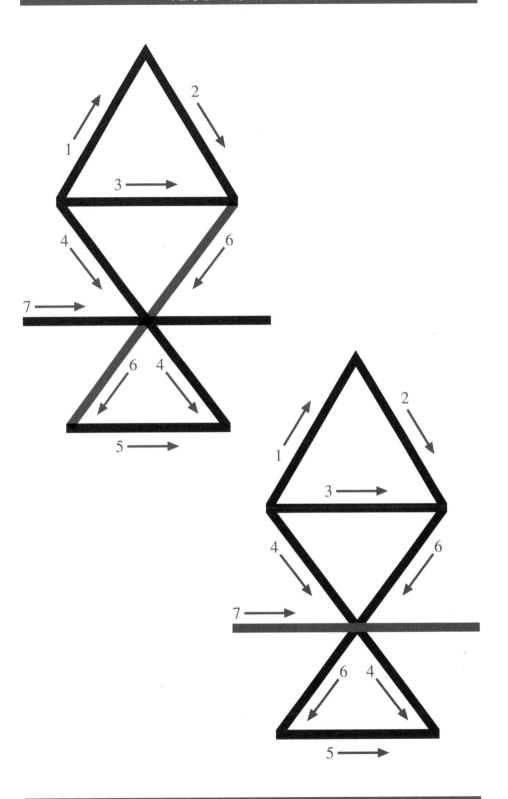

Hand Placements

Hand placements are included in the "technical" part of Reiki. Many people who engage in Reiki claim that there is actually no importance to hand placements – everyone can place his hands wherever he wants on his or someone else's body, and in every way, as long as he does not harm himself or anyone else. This is not Master Naharo's opinion .

Master Naharo sees Reiki as a life art that is meant for everyone, and as such it has to adhere to a number of rules. Just as a person who wishes to participate in a dance must learn the dance steps in order to fit in with the rest of the dancers, so a person who wants to participate in Reiki has to learn the way to hold his hand, the various ways of placing his hands, the location of the various placements, and their sequence.

Master Naharo developed many precise methods for placing hands, some of which are meant for self-treatment and some for treating others.

We will first explain the great importance of the correct position of the hands in every placement. Then we will present 22 basic hand placements for self-treatment, as well as several comments regarding the application of the placement of hands in treating other people, in sending long-distance Reiki, or in treating animals. Finally, we will present 20 different detailed Reiki self-treatment procedures.

In addition to the rules for the hand placements, Master Naharo determined various links between hand placements and their location, and the healing points in the human body (the Marma points). Since every Marma point is linked to diseases, conditions of stress, physical systems, and various energetic blockages and imbalances, the links present the reader with knowledge that connects the hand placements to the possibility of healing and treating the problem or blockage in the body's systems. (In the appendix at the end of the book, all the Marma points appear in their conventional order, and each one is explained.)

In the process of enlightenment (sometimes also called channeling), Master Naharo found the links between the 12 basic Reiki symbols and the 22 basic Reiki hand placements. The master attributed three symbols to each of the placements. There is no point seeking logic or causality in these links – they were given to the Master by a superior enlightened force, and he taught his pupils what he had learned from God. Learn the symbols connected with each placement, and in that way you can increase the effect of Reiki tenfold.

We will present each of the 22 basic placements with an illustration, a photograph, an explanation of the Marma points connected to the placement and its location, and information about the placements, their duration, and the required pressure, as well as the symbols that enhance the positive action of the placement.

The principle of holding the hand

In the center of the palm, there is a point the size of a small coin. This point is located in the concave part of the palm, at a distance of approximately two finger-widths from the junction of the ring finger and the middle finger. Everyone should get to know this point well, since besides its being the opening of the pipe of Reiki energy, it is also (perhaps as a result) a point that stimulates sexuality and vitality. In other words, when we activate Reiki energy, this energy flows from a little point in the center of the palm, and from there it passes and flows to other places in the body (either of the person who is treating himself or of the recipient).

For this reason, the hand is held in two basic ways:

1. When the palm is held so that it is touching some part of the body, as if to join the opening of the pipe in its center to the opening of another pipe in the body – the hand is flat and adapts to the surface of the body part it is touching.

2. When the hand is cupped, and the Reiki energy is sent from the end of the pipe, traverses a short distance in the air (in self-treatment) or a long distance in the air (long-distance treatment), and penetrates the body of the practitioner or the recipient – the hand is a bit curved, as if to concentrate and focus the energy that is flowing out of the opening. Here we must add a few words about cupped hands and curved hands. In various Reiki books, these contradictory terms are used to apply to the same thing. Cupped hands relate to a hollow in the center of the hand, such as when we scoop up water in order to sip it. If we invert the hand, the back of the hand is convex, that is, it looks like a little hill or dome. The situation and position of the palm have not changed – only our point of view has changed (as in the case of speaking about ascending or descending a slope, when it is actually a matter of which direction we are facing). Since Master Naharo sees the interior of the hand as the important part in projecting Reiki, we will relate to the hands that serve us by transmitting Reiki as *cupped*.

Later on, instructions regarding the hand placements are given. In cases in which detailed instructions are not given, the practitioner must rely on his instincts and work according to their directives. This will most likely be the most suitable way for him.

In conclusion, some advice collected by Gail Radford regarding the hand placement is presented here – advice that neither replaces nor contradicts Master Naharo's instructions, but simply explains them in the spirit of the West. This brief explanation is not a substitute for the chapters of the course in detail that follow. However, it is important since it elucidates the process and focuses the attention on the importance of the hands during Reiki.

During Reiki treatment, the hands must face downward – as far as possible – with fingers close together, slightly cupped. That is, the hands are parallel to the ground as much as possible. This situation may change in various therapeutic positions or in self-administered Reiki.

When placing your hands on your own or the recipient's body, do not press hard, but just place them gently.

Both hands are placed simultaneously on the part of the body being treated, taking care not to cross the arms.

When a "double" area is mentioned, such as the shoulders, one hand is placed on each shoulder.

It is also possible to place one hand after the other if necessary or if it is more comfortable, but under no circumstances must one hand be placed on top of the other.

When we want to place the hand on a sensitive area, such as the groin, we do not place it physically on the area, because of its sensitivity, but hold it at a distance of 5-7 cm (2-2.5 inches) above the area. In self-treatment, this limitation does not exist.

It is possible, and sometimes desirable, not to physically place the hands in Reiki (in self-treatment, too), but rather to hold them at a distance of 5-7 cm above the body. In this way, people who shy away from any kind of contact with the opposite sex for religious or other reasons can avail themselves of Reiki treatment with impunity, since the treatment can be performed without physical contact.

When Reiki is performed using hand placements, we must remember an important point: not to break contact with the recipient's body during the passage from one placement point to the next. It is very important to see that there is constant contact.

When we want to move from one point to another, we first move one hand to the next point, while the other hand is still on the previous point, and then move the second hand as well.

When we change position, or when we ask the recipient to turn over, that is, to move from a supine to a prone position and so on, it is advisable to leave one or both hands lying gently on a certain point on the body during the turn in order not to break the contact.

If for some reason it is not possible to leave our hand on the recipient's body during the change of position, it is important to leave the hand there "in spirit" – either on the body or on the area of its aura.

The same is also true, of course, in a treatment in which, for some reason, the practitioner cannot place his hands on the recipient's body.

When the treatment is over, the hands must not be removed from the recipient's body in a sharp, abrupt movement, but rather very slowly, in a gentle movement. There are masters who teach various finishing movements. One of them, which is very common, is a movement that is similar to the "time out" movement in basketball, and its purpose is to announce, from the energetic point of view, that the treatment has been completed. This is also true, of course, for self-treatment.

The 22 Basic Reiki Placements According to Master Naharo

1 Hands on your head – one, two, three

This is the most basic placement from which it is actually possible to learn the nature of Reiki in its entirety. When we see this position for the first time, the thought, "Oh no, something had has happened" occurs to us – but such a thought is opposed to both the nature of Reiki and to the basic principles of Reiki that we have learned.

Placement number 1 provides the first link to Reiki. Sit straight-backed or stand with your feet close together. Bring your hands, facing upward, to below the center of your chest, arms bent. From this point, after taking a deep breath, lift your hands and place them on your head, like in the picture. Your elbows face outward (with no exertion), your thumbs are close to your hands, your wrists are near your ears without touching them.

Your hands exert a steady, medium pressure on your head. Although they are slightly cupped, their entire length touches your head, without any gap. The duration of the placement is about three minutes. Breathing must be steady and natural.

During the course of the placement, it is a good idea to meditate and see in your mind's eye the tremendous power of the Reiki energy as a huge sheet of water that is flowing from the top of the sky onto the earth like an infinite waterfall, whose breadth and height cannot be measured.

At the end of the placement, bring your hands back to the starting position (opposite your chest), and then straighten your arms and shake them lightly.

The Marma points that are affected during the placement are 11, 51, and 52 (for a full explanation of the Marma points, see the appendix at the end of the book).

The symbols that increase the beneficial effect of this placement are number 3 – Hun-Sha-Zi-Shu-Neen, number 6 – Rakku, and number 9 – To-Ho.

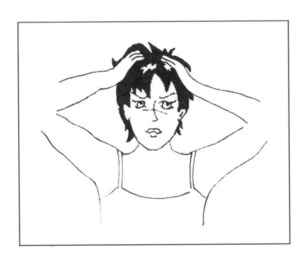

2 A hat made of hands – the tired person gathers strength

The second placement is also a very basic position, and some people begin the sequence of hand placements with this one. It is called "a hat" since it imitates the customary head covering in Poonah, the seat of Master Naharo – a hat from which a fabric covering flows down the neck.

Placement number 2 affords a link to Reiki energy as well as quick charging of energy in a body that lacks energy. In contrast to the first Reiki position, which is easy and performed naturally and correctly, the second position is not natural, and you must ensure that you perform it accurately.

Hold your hands in the basic position, with your hands turned upward and held opposite your chest. You can either sit straight-backed or stand up straight with your legs close together. Take a deep breath, raise your hands in a broad movement, and place your hands on your head. Your elbows face outward (without exertion). Your right hand is higher up, and it covers the crown of your head. Your fingers are open. Your thumb does not touch the other fingers. Your left hand is on the nape of your neck. There is no contact between your two hands. Your left thumb is close to your hand. Your right hand presses lightly on your head, your left hand presses slightly harder. Important: There is no contact between your two hands, either while raising them or while placing them.

The duration of the placement is about two minutes. During that time, it is very important not to feel as if your head is being pushed forward (this would indicate that your left hand is pressing your head too hard). Your inhalation is deep and your exhalation is long and slow. During the course of the placement, it is a good idea to meditate and to see in your mind's eye the gigantic sun rising in the east, giving off light and heat, and gradually appearing over the horizon.

At the end of the placement, straighten your arms, bring your hands back to the starting position, and then shake them lightly. You can also pass your hands over your head and neck in light "shampooing" movements.

The Marma point that is affected during the placement is 52 (for a full explanation of the Marma points, see the appendix at the end of the book).

The symbols that increase the beneficial effect of this placement are number 1 – Cho-Ko-Rey, number 5 – Dai-Ku-Myo, and number 8 – Saa-Saa.

3 The head triangle (or the upper triangle) – entreaty to the superior force

Placement number 3 is called "triangle" because of the shape that is formed by your two hands. This placement apparently originated from the position of the hands during prayer, but in Reiki it developed in a different way than in other religions.

The starting position of placement number 3 is, as in the two previous ones, with your hands turned upward opposite your chest. Your body is straight (sitting or standing). From this position, raise your arms upward and place your hands on your head, with your fingers together, as in the picture. Your hands are slightly cupped, so that there is a small gap between your hands and your head, but it is important that your fingertips press on your head (the root of your hands touches your head lightly). Your elbows face outward and slightly forward. The fingers of your two hands are touching, and the resulting shape is of an upward-facing triangle.

There are no time limits for this placement, and the only limit is that in this position, quite naturally, the head is pressed forward a little. In order to counteract this push, your shoulder-blades pull your back backward. When you feel tension in the body as a result of this pushing/pulling, it's time to stop the placement.

Placement number 3 serves as a personal expression of the link with the general Reiki energy – that is, when the practitioner submits a personal entreaty to the unlimited universal force. The meditation that is performed during this placement is also personal – for instance, the practitioner can raise a problem that is bothering him in his mind's eye and see, through meditation, the problem "erased" by a stream of blue water or by a wave of golden light.

At the end of the placement, lower your hands to your sides, and shake your body a bit to relax the tension.

The Marma point that is affected during the placement is 10 (for a full explanation of the Marma points, see the appendix at the end of the book).

The symbols that increase the beneficial effect of this placement are number 2 – Se-He-Key, number 6 – Rakku, and number 10 – Zonar.

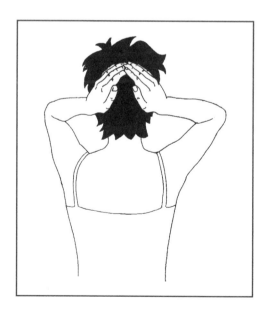

4 Overlapping – facing the entire world with head held straight

Placement number 4 is a slightly different one. Although we place our hands on our neck, as will be described, the head is responsible for doing most of the "work," since it is cradled in the hands and rubs against them.

Sit or stand straight with your legs together. Lift your hands above your head and lower your right hand onto the back of your neck. Lower your left hand onto the right hand and grasp them above the palm and below the thumb (as in the picture). Your elbows face outward. Now press your grasped overlapping hands against the back of your neck.

Now a little struggle begins. Your hands push forward, and your head pushes back against them. It is important to keep your head erect, and not let it "fall" forward.

Maintain this position for 3-5 minutes. During the course of the placement, the meditation that is performed is personal – the practitioner must identify the problem that is bothering him the most (depression, an inability to form a relationship, weak energy, bashfulness, a particular allergy, and so on) and simply "wash" it in the tremendous stream of blue water or golden light, or make it disappear in the big green expanse that is growing opposite his eyes.

This is a very effective placement, which creates a strong link with Reiki energy.

After the placement, shake your arms well and turn your neck from side to side in order to relax the pressure that was created in it as a result of an as yet imperfect performance of the exercise. (After some time, you will learn to balance the pushing and pulling, and the tension in your neck will disappear.)

It is an excellent placement to perform – on its own, not as part of a set of placements – upon getting up in the morning.

The Marma point that is affected during the placement is 10 (for a full explanation of the Marma points, see the appendix at the end of the book).

The symbols that increase the beneficial effect of this placement are number 3 – Hun-Sha-Zi-Shu-Neen, number 5 – Dai-Ku-Myo, and number 11 – Har-Te.

5 Capping the eyes – seeing without seeing

Placement number 5, capping the eyes (covering them as if with caps), is a placement or position that appears almost naturally in various situations in human life. Tired people or confused people who cannot concentrate place their hands in this position naturally in order to calm down. People who are sad or in a crisis cover their eyes in this way.

Placement number 5 begins with your arms straight and your palms facing your body. Lift your hands while bending your arms and place your right hand over your right eye and your left hand over your left eye. There is no contact between your hands, and the bridge of your nose serves as a boundary between your hands. Your nose and mouth remain uncovered. Your fingers and thumbs are closed, and your hand is slightly cupped (like a dome). Exert light pressure. Your head leans forward slightly in order to merge with your hands. Your eyes can be open or closed. (In general, if you keep your eyes open at the beginning of the exercise, they close during the course of it.)

This placement can be done for quite a long time – even up to 10 minutes.

During the course of the placement, you can perform a prolonged meditation. Generally speaking, Reiki masters recommend performing a "joyful" meditation during the placement – that is, think about something that gladdens your heart, and drench it in golden light in order to intensify the happiness.

At the end of the placement, remove your hands and blink your eyes a few times. Rub your hands together (as if washing them) and shake them lightly.

The Marma points that are affected during the placement are 4 and 50 (for a full explanation of the Marma points, see the appendix at the end of the book).

The symbols that increase the beneficial effect of this placement are number 1 – Cho-Ko-Rey, number 7 – Rakku-An, and number 12 – Ha-Loo.

6 A "slap" on the cheeks – to arouse the self

Placement number 6 is short and meaningful, and its purpose is to stimulate the flow of energy in the body. You should do this placement standing up.

Hold your arms straight at your sides, your hands facing your body. Lift your hands until they are opposite your chest, and rub them against each other. As a direct continuation of the movement, bend your arms to form a right angle with your armpits and "slap" your hands (very lightly) on the cheeks. Your fingers are closed, and your thumbs are held tightly against your hands and do not touch your ear. The placement continues for a short time only. During the course of the placement, you perform a meditation called "It's not so terrible." You think of a "disaster" that happened to you (for example, the egg that was supposed to be sunny-side-up turned into an unidentifiable mess in the pan), and wash the "disaster" away in a wave of yellow-green splendor.

At the end of the placement, rub your hands together again and shake them, as if shaking water off them.

The Marma points that are affected during the placement are 47, 48, and 49 (for a full explanation of the Marma points, see the appendix at the end of the book).

The symbols that increase the beneficial effect of this placement are number 2 – Se-He-Key, number 7 – Rakku-An, and number 8 – Saa-Saa.

Take note – the practitioner or the therapist must stick to the principles of hand placements, but he may sometimes feel that he must change the placement position slightly. This is not a problem. It is true of the practitioner whose photos appear in this book – her instincts sometimes dictated that she deviate slightly from the exact hand placements.

7 Pressing the temples – concentrating your thoughts

Placement number 7 is an important and fundamental Reiki placement, and it serves to make large amounts of Reiki energy flow quickly to the energetic body.

This placement can be performed in any position – standing, sitting, or lying on your back.

Hold your arms straight at your sides, your hands facing your body. Lift your hands until they are opposite your chest, and rub them against each other. As a direct continuation of the movement, bend your arms and bring your hands up to your cheeks (as in placement number 6). Move your elbows downward toward your body until they are against your chest (in contrast to placement number 6). Your fingers are close together, and your fingertips press your temples hard (the thumb does not take part in this pressure).

This placement is performed for brief periods of time (1-2 minutes), but very intensely. During the placement, which serves mainly to acquire the ability to concentrate and focus, perform a meditation of contemplation: Choose a particular object (such as a flower) and focus on one of its parts (a petal). Scrutinize the part as if through a magnifying glass, and with each progressive stage of the magnification, focus on a smaller part of the petal.

It is very important to ensure that you breathe regularly throughout the placement.

Remember that pressure on the temples that is too strong can be harmful, and can even lead to fainting.

At the end of the placement, rub your hands together once more and shake them, as if shaking water off them.

The Marma points that are affected during the placement are 48 and 49 (for a full explanation of the Marma points, see the appendix at the end of the book).

The symbols that increase the beneficial effect of this placement are number 3 – Hun-Sha-Zi-Shu-Neen, number 6 – Rakku, and number 11 – Har-Te.

8 The back triangle – erect posture

Placement number 8 is a popular placement or position in many therapy methods. Its main objective is to cause the Reiki energy to flow to the lower chakras (from the base chakra to the heart chakra), which are considered more "physical," and therefore it is difficult for them to open up to Reiki energy.

This placement is performed sitting or standing. Hold your arms straight out in front of you, your palms facing upward. Lift your arms (which are still straight) above your head, and then bend your elbows and bring your hands to your back, to the area of the shoulder-blades. Try to create the shape of a triangle with your fingers. Your three middle fingers press your body as hard as possible, while your thumbs and pinkies just touch it. Your elbows are raised up high. Your gaze is forward.

This placement is performed for about three minutes, exerting as strong a pressure as possible.

During the course of the placement, perform a brief meditation that focuses on your self-worth. You must see yourself as you want to be – successful, strong, handsome, and so on – and envelop yourself in golden light that streams from the sun or from some other source of light.

At the end of the placement, straighten your arms, twist them around once or twice (in order to relax the shoulders and the shoulder-blades), and shake them in a downward direction.

The Marma points that are affected during the placement are 45 and 46 (for a full explanation of the Marma points, see the appendix at the end of the book).

The symbols that increase the beneficial effect of this placement are number 1 – Cho-Ko-Rey, number 5 – Dai-Ku-Myo, and number 12 – Ha-Loo.

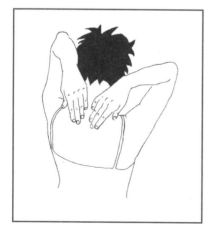

9 Closing a circle – self-expression

Placement number 9 is sometimes called "the choking position" (as is position number 10), but perceiving it as choking is a distortion of the entire picture. The opposite is true. Placement number 9 actually closes the hands in a circle around the neck – or more precisely surrounds the column of the chakras – and enables the Reiki energy to flow in a circular, spiral movement inside the person's body. A spiral movement of energy in the energetic body and around the chakras creates a situation in which the person expresses himself on a higher plane; in other words, he attains more powerful self-expression.

The placement can be performed for quite a long time. The pressure is weak. This is one of the only placements in which the arms (but not the hands) may touch each other.

This placement is performed sitting or standing, but never lying down!

Stretch your arms out in front of you at shoulder height. Your hands face downward. Bring your hands to your neck while bending your arms and placing your elbows as close to your chest as possible. Place your cupped hands (fingers close together) on your neck.

The best meditation for this placement is the ladder meditation. See yourself climbing up a large, solid ladder, with each rung glowing with a more resplendent light than the previous rung. As you ascend the ladder (during the meditation), you become more and more glowing.

At the end of the placement, shake your hands and then rub your neck (as if washing it) with your hands.

Take care not to press on your neck – this placement is meant to close a circle and not to choke you!

The Marma points that are affected during the placement are 12 and 13 (for a full explanation of the Marma points, see the appendix at the end of the book).

The symbols that increase the beneficial effect of this placement are number 2 – Se-He-Key, number 7 – Rakku-An, and number 11 – Har-Te.

10 Lifting the chin – improving self-esteem

Placement number 10, despite the fact that it is located on the neck and upper chest, also affects the position of the chin, and this is where its name comes from. This placement can be performed for a long time. The pressure exerted by the left hand is weak and the pressure exerted by the right hand is strong.

The placement is performed sitting or standing, not lying down. The starting position is when both hands are held in front of the body, the palms facing upward. First lift your left hand and place it on your neck, the thumb to the left and your fingers to the right. Your fingers push your neck so that the back of your hand pushes your jaw and chin upward a bit. The center point of your hand is located opposite your windpipe. After you have placed your left hand, lift your right hand and place it on your upper chest, fingers slightly apart, beneath your left arm. Your breathing must be normal and regular. Do not close your eyes in this placement.

The meditation associated with this placement must be a meditation of thanks – giving thanks to someone or something that has effected a change for the better in your life: parents, partner, God, and so on.

After this placement, it is very important to walk around for a minute or two while shaking your arms downward.

The Marma points that are affected during the placement are 5, 6, and 14 (for a full explanation of the Marma points, see the appendix at the end of the book).

The symbols that increase the beneficial effect of this placement are number 3 – Hun-Sha-Zi-Shu-Neen, number 6 – Rakku, and number 9 – To-Ho.

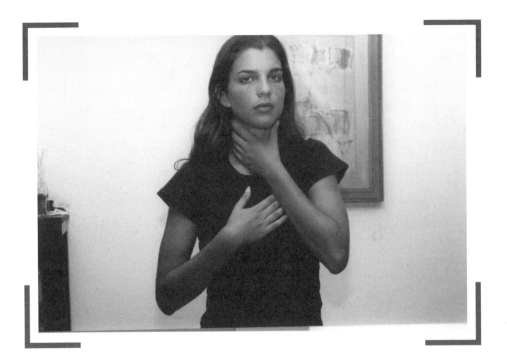

11 The (upper) chest placement – the key to happiness

Placement number 11 is a basic placement, slightly similar to placement number 1 in that it constitutes a direct and rapid opening to Reiki energy. With the help of the appropriate symbols, it is possible to channel with Reiki energy any time, any place, and receive within a very short time an "infusion" of refreshing and invigorating energy. This placement can be performed in any position of the body. Master Naharo is in the habit of performing this placement during self-treatment while he is floating on his back in the river!

The starting position of the body is when your arms are held straight at your sides. First lift your left hand and place it on the location as in the picture. Lift your right hand and add it to the placement. Watch out for the placement of your right thumb – it must point upward. The placement is performed with the same medium pressure exerted by both hands.

Master Naharo proposes a meditation that is called "The bucket that is never emptied" during this placement. In your mind's eye, see a bucket that you want to fill with water. Now fill the bucket with clear water (identical to Reiki energy in your mind). Imagine an infinite waterfall pouring into the bucket. Although there are no holes in the bucket, is not full, and the water does not overflow from it. Continue doing this for a few minutes. At the end of the meditation, take the bucket with you (in your mind's eye) wherever you go.

At the end of the placement, shake your arms and rub your hands together.

This placement, number 11, is an extremely powerful one, and has many uses.

The Marma points that are affected during the placement are 14, 17, and 18 (for a full explanation of the Marma points, see the appendix at the end of the book).

The symbols that increase the beneficial effect of this placement are number 4 – Di-Ko-Myo, number 5 – Dai-Ku-Miyo, and number 12 – Ha-Loo.

12 Upper abdomen – existence

Placement number 12 is a basic placement, extremely important, that is always performed standing up. (Only in the case of a person who for some reason cannot stand, is it performed sitting down.) This placement "refuels" the Reiki energy in the human energetic body, and for this reason it is advisable to perform it on a regular basis, once or twice a day, at fixed times. The use of meditation on one of the symbols associated with this hand placement increases the flow of Reiki to the human "container" (remember – there is no problem of excessive Reiki, so that the container never actually overflows).

The starting position is when the body is erect. Your hands are held in front of the chest, touching each other, elbows bent. The thumbs and fingers of one hand press against the thumb and fingers of the other hand. From this starting position, move your hands to the area of your upper abdomen (the diaphragm) with your elbows facing outward and your arms in a straight line, as far as possible. Your fingers are close together (on each hand) and your fingertips are touching. Your thumbs are separate from your fingers and parallel to them. Your fingers press gently on your upper abdomen. Your breathing must be deep, so that you feel your inhalation and exhalation in your hands. Do not close your eyes during this placement, which can be lengthy – up to seven minutes.

The meditation performed during the placement concerns the chakras in the human body (a more detailed explanation of the chakras appears in the relevant chapter in this book). The central chakras are seven wheels of energy that serve as openings for the various kinds of energy of the body (the aura), and they are arrange on a column that is parallel to the spinal column. Each of the seven chakras is linked directly to a different body system, body parts, and existential plane. You must visualize the chakra in which you feel you have problems or blockages. (In other words, the field for which the chakra is responsible is "defective" in you.) At the beginning of the placement, you must visualize the chakra as a wheel spinning slowly on an axis. Then you must imagine a stream or ray of light (preferably in a color that suits the basic color of the chakra) drenching the wheel and beginning to spin it faster and faster. It is the stream of Reiki energy that penetrates the "problematic" chakra and purifies it. At the end of the meditation, you must stop the stream of light and "turn off the faucet."

At the end of the placement, it is important to shake your arms and rub your hands together. You should walk around a bit in order to get your breathing back to its normal rate.

The Marma points that are affected during the placement are 19 and 20 (for a full explanation of the Marma points, see the appendix at the end of the book).

The symbols that increase the beneficial effect of this placement are number 1 – Cho-Ko-Rey, number 7 – Rakku-An, and number 11 – Har-Te.

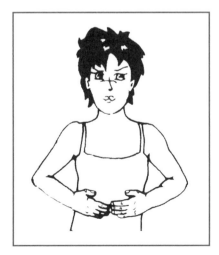

13 Lower abdomen – continuity

Placement number 13 is actually linked to placement number 12, and it is performed in a similar manner except that your hands are placed lower (that is, there is hardly any angle in your arms – they are almost straight), and your thumbs are turned slightly downward.

This placement is called "continuity," and Master Naharo explains that this continuity is linked to the concept of "nutrition." In the same way that the body needs food and water for ongoing nutrition, so it also needs to be fed Reiki energy constantly for its existence. Many people, including those who do not practice Reiki, are in the habit of naturally holding their hands in a way that resembles placement number 13 – they are requesting Reiki nutrition unconsciously. (It is important to remember that this unconscious placement sometimes occurs when lying on one's back or while sleeping, while conscious Reiki prefers the standing position or – if necessary – the sitting position.)

You can perform placement number 13 on its own or as a direct continuation of placement number 12. (It is not a good idea to go from placement number 13 to placement number 12, but it is possible in certain cases, and of course it does not do any harm under any circumstances.) If you go directly from placement number 12 to placement number 13, you must ensure that your hands (at least one of them) remain in contact with your body all the time.

The recommended meditation for this placement is also connected to the column of the chakras, except that this time the stream of light – the Reiki energy – is poured like a waterfall onto the column of the chakras, and revolves the dysfunctional chakra/s in a way that it considers best. (Reiki energy knows what the person needs better than the person himself does.)

At the end of the placement, which can take five or even seven minutes, you must rub your entire abdomen with both hands – men in a clockwise direction and women in an anti-clockwise direction – and shake your hands and arms as if after washing them.

The Marma points that are affected during the placement are 21 and 22 (for a full explanation of the Marma points, see the appendix at the end of the book).

The symbols that increase the beneficial effect of this placement are number 2 – Se-He-Key, number 6 – Rakku, and number 12 – Ha-Loo.

14 Thumb on the navel – linking

Placement number 14 is a slightly "strange" placement. Although, like all the other Reiki placements, it causes Reiki to flow from the outside inward to the person's body, this placement also makes the Reiki energy that is already inside the body flow. It is a mistake to think that the Reiki energy, when it reaches the person's body, divides up equally among all of his organs and systems. This is not the case. There are organs in which there is a lack of Reiki. (As we mentioned before, there is never a problem of an excess of Reiki.) This placement is mainly meant to cause the Reiki energy to flow to places where it is lacking, the Reiki that is conveyed being taken from the reservoir of Reiki energy that exists in the body itself.

This placement can be performed standing or lying down (not sitting, since sitting distorts the shape of the body and moves the hands out of the correct position). The starting position is when the arms are straight down at your sides, hands facing your body. First, bring your right hand to your body and place it, open-fingered, on your abdomen, with the tip of your thumb placed exactly on your navel and your pinkie on your pubic region. Add your left hand, with closed fingers, your left thumb touching your right pinkie. The pressure of the placement is gentle, and breathing is natural. When you perform this placement lying down, you can close your eyes. There is no time limit to this placement.

The meditation that is associated with this placement is rather complicated, and you may occasionally have some difficulty evoking it in your mind's eye. We will just give general directions here. You must see yourself as your are in your mind's eye. After you have done this, drench the image in white, shining light, and safeguard it like this – an image of yourself in your mind's eye, enveloped in shining light. Now evoke the image of yourself as a child in your mind's eye, in another situation, in another period of your life (the choice is personal), and draw this second image into the shining image of yourself, until it is assimilated inside it. In this way, you can draw an infinite number of images of yourself into the shining image. At the end of the process, "scramble" the shining image until it disappears as a point of light into the infinite expanse of the universe.

At the end of the placement, shake your arms and legs.

The Marma point that is affected during the placement is 22 (for a full explanation of the Marma points, see the appendix at the end of the book).

The symbols that increase the beneficial effect of this placement are number 3 – Hun-Sha-Zi-Shu-Neen, number 5 – Dai-Ku-Myo, and number 8 – Saa-Saa.

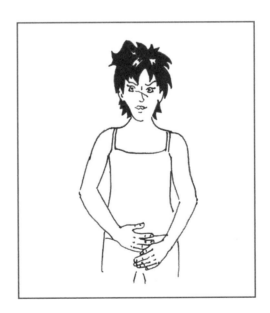

The right and left hands can be used interchangeably in this placement.

15 Lower triangle (the pubic triangle) – lust

Placement number 15 is called "lust," and sometimes Reiki practitioners (especially of Western origin) remark that lust is incongruous with pure, pristine Reiki. In their eyes, lust is connected to some kind of "perversion" or unacceptable behavior. This is not the case in Master Naharo's eyes. According to him, lust is "the glue that unites a man and a woman, a person and his goal, members of a community and the individual in the universe." Lust is what motivates a person to get up in the morning and fulfill his duties to himself, his family, and his entire community. Lust is what causes parents to sacrifice themselves – in one way or another – for the sake of a good future for their children: the lust to see with their own eyes their offspring growing and thriving. When you engage in Reiki, and in this placement, you must remember the meaning of lust in this context.

This placement is performed standing or lying on your back (not sitting). You can do it for up to seven minutes, exerting fairly strong, steady pressure.

The starting position for this placement is when you hold your arms straight at your sides, your hands facing your body. At the first stage, lift your arms and let your hands touch each other opposite your chest, your elbows touching your body. Let your thumbs touch the rest of your fingers (and leave them closed for the entire duration). Put your hands on your body in the area of the upper abdomen, fingers pointing downward, and slide them downward, gently rubbing until you reach the position of the pubic triangle shown in the picture. Your arms are straight or slightly bent at the elbows. Your thumbs (sometimes some of the fingers, too) touch each other.

Master Naharo calls the meditation associated with this placement "the blooming of the lotus." You must evoke your "lust" in your mind's eye. This could be a lust of any kind, including a lust for a man or a woman, for material success or for good health. In your mind's eye, shape your "lust" as a little plant, which you irrigate with golden light that flows (in your mind's eye) from a little stream. The little plant grows into a big, green, blooming tree, until its fruit emerges from among the leaves, round and red like the fruit of paradise. (In Indian traditions, the fruit of sacred trees is red and round, like apples.) If you are an experienced practitioner, you can also meditate about the fruit and see yourself stretching out your hand, plucking the fruit, and eating it.

At the end of the placement (which can take a long time), you must pull your hands to your upper abdomen, and from that point relax them and your arms by shaking them gently.

General comment: Some of the placements, especially the last ones, involve touching the sexual organs, such as the breasts or the pubic region. In self-administered Reiki, there are no limitations. However, when you are treating another person, there is the danger of undesirable contact that is manipulative by nature. Later on we will see how each of the various placements is performed when the treatment is not self-administered (and we will observe that there are a number of methods, and in fact every experienced Reiki practitioner can determine the exact method of placing hands for himself, relying on a few simple rules). Here it is important to observe that Reiki is not a form of sexual contact – even when intimate relations exist between practitioner and recipient (such as when a wife gives her husband Reiki energy). If the practitioner finds it difficult to draw a clear distinction between sexuality and Reiki, it would be better for him to perform Reiki in sensitive areas with his hands at a distance of about five centimeters from the areas, his flat hand facing the recipient's body. As we know, Reiki is performed fully clothed (as is self-administered Reiki) – both practitioner and recipient.

The Marma point that is affected during the placement is 22 (for a full explanation of the Marma points, see the appendix at the end of the book).

The symbols that increase the beneficial effect of this placement are number 4 – Di-Ko-Miyo, number 7 – Rakku-An, and number 10 – Zonar.

16 Straightening the spinal column – self-confidence

Placement number 16 is the first of three placements that treat the lower back and the tailbone, and are in fact meant to strengthen the lower spine and the three lower chakras. These are extremely important placements, and are sometimes performed sequentially (16, 17, 18). They are considered to be the Reiki placements with the most powerful physical therapeutic ability. It goes without saying that these placements appear naturally in various people, even without Reiki practice or awareness.

This placement is performed standing, and it can also be performed sitting (on a chair without a back). If you sit, you must ensure that your legs do not touch each other and that they are not crossed. There is no time limit. However, you should not spend more than seven minutes doing it. The pressure exerted is quite strong.

The starting position is when your arms are bent and your hands are next to each other in prayer position. Your elbows are close to your body. After taking a deep breath, bring your hands to the back of your waist, as in the picture. The height of your hands is not fixed, but your middle fingers should be approximately "opposite" your navel. Your thumbs do not touch the other fingers, and face downward. Your hands can be slightly cupped. You should try to ensure that your hands are in line with each other, but this is not mandatory.

Your arms are bent and your elbows are as far as possible from your body.

It is important to check your breathing cycle: when inhaling, your fingers and thumbs "push" your body forward (as if on a hinge, when your hands do not participate in the pushing); when exhaling, your fingers draw away in a backward direction.

The meditation that is suitable for this placement is the one called "the seed." This meditation is directed at the seed that is buried in the person's past, or even in his karma, which affects (adversely) his subconscious in the present. In general, people do not expose this seed consciously, and are sometimes not even completely aware of its existence. The process of meditation, which is performed in a personal way, with everyone doing it in the way he wants, uncovers the seed in a morass of mud at the bottom of a murky lake. Two waterfalls – one of pure, clear water and the other of golden light – pour into the murky lake, and the combination of the water and the light slowly cleans the lake. The water becomes clear, the mud disappears – and at the bottom of the lake the person sees – or more importantly, identifies – the seed that contributed to his lack of self-confidence.

Placement number 16 and the meditation associated with it go on for some time, according to your feeling. At the end, gather up the seed to your heart (the heart chakra), rub your hands up and down over your body, and shake your arms.

If you go on to placement number 17, do not detach your hands from your body, but slide them downward to the next placement.

The Marma points that are affected during the placement are 41, 42, and 43, 44 (for a full explanation of the Marma points, see the appendix at the end of the book).

The symbols that increase the beneficial effect of this placement are number 1 – Cho-Ko-Rey, number 6 – Rakku, and number 11 – Har-Te.

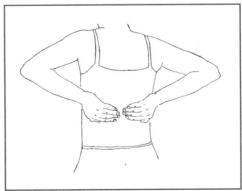

17 Consolidating the spine – grounding

Placement number 17 is actually the continuation of placement number 16, except that it deals with consolidating the practitioner's self-confidence. In fact, we can say that after exposing the "seed" in placement number 16, we take the seed in this placement and turn it into part of the reservoir that nourishes the column of the chakras.

If you perform this placement after placement number 16, slide your hands downward until you reach the position in the picture. Your arms are still bent, and can also be straight. In parallel, continue with the previous meditation. Instead of pulling the seed to the heart chakra, bury it at the base of the spine, the base chakra.

If placement number 17 is performed independently (and not as a continuation of number 16), the starting position is identical, and your hands are placed on your buttocks, your fingers pointing downwards and your thumbs next to them (not forcibly). There is no time limit for the placement.

The meditation is similar to the meditation for placement number 16, except that in its second part (after the seed has been uncovered), you bury the seed at the base of the "tree" of the chakras.

The end of the placement is similar to that of number 16. If you continue on to placement number 18, do not detach your hands from your body. (It is not customary to go from placement 17 to 16. The direction is downward, toward the earth, which grounds.)

The Marma points that are affected during the placement are 39 and 40 (for a full explanation of the Marma points, see the appendix at the end of the book).

The symbols that increase the beneficial effect of this placement are number 2 – Se-He-Key, number 5 – Dai-Ku-Myo, and number 12 – Ha-Loo.

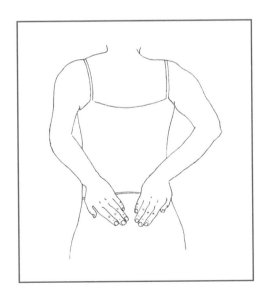

18 The triangle of the buttocks – grounding

Placement number 18 is actually the "end" of the process that began with placement number 16. The meaning of grounding is that the person buries the seed he found at the bottom of the muddy lake and makes it a part of himself, that is, a conscious part of his being.

You can reach placement number 18 directly from number 16 or 17, or you can reach it from the starting position. In this placement, your fingers are close together, your thumbs facing "outward." The triangle that is created faces downward (parallel to the crack in your bottom), the pressure is strong, and the duration of the placement is lengthy.

In parallel, the meditation is a continuation of the meditation for placements number 16 and 17 (even if you start directly with number 18). After you bury the seed at the base of the tree of the chakras, you continue to nourish the seed with golden light and clear water so that the meditation "explains" what the subconscious exposes in terms that the conscious can absorb.

The end of the placement is similar to the end of placements number 16 and 17.

We will comment once more: The three last placements are generally performed in one continuum. When you go from one placement to the next, the transition is always downward (that is, toward the ground).

The Marma point that is affected during the placement is 40 (for a full explanation of the Marma points, see the appendix at the end of the book).

The symbols that increase the beneficial effect of this placement are number 3 – Hun-Sha-Zi-Shu-Neen, number 7 – Rakku-An, and number 11 – Har-Te.

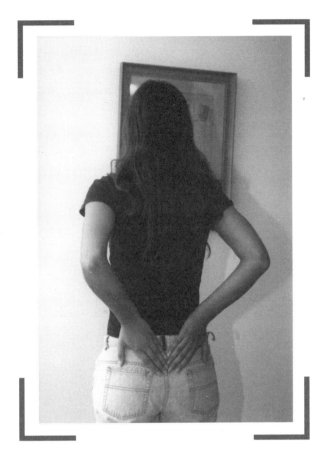

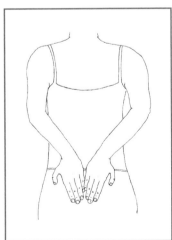

19 Holding the knees – movement

Placement number 19 is performed in a sitting position only, straight-backed, head up, facing forward, arms straight and hands placed on the knees, fingers and thumbs close together and facing downward. Your hands are slightly cupped. Your right hand is on your right knee and your left hand is on your left knee. There is no crossing. The pressure is hard and there is no time limit.

In fact, there is no starting position for placement number 19. You sit down and arrange your body until you reach the correct position, and then you begin to get the Reiki energy to flow.

This placement treats problems of movement – this could be physical movement of the body, or the person's movement from one situation to another or from place to place, or inner movement (toward a state of enlightenment).

Master Naharo recommends that meditation not be performed in this placement. We feel that sitting in this position, looking straight ahead, leads to natural meditation (usually the kind that arises and purifies the practitioner's current problems in his mind's eye).

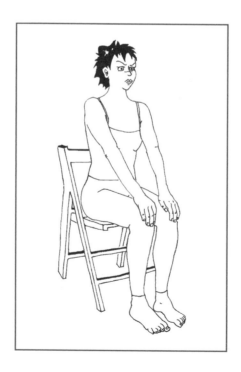

Another way of performing placement number 19 is when both hands are placed on the same knee, first on the left knee, and then on the right. Both hands are cupped, and the fingers are free, as are the thumbs. Your body bends slightly toward the knee that is being treated.

At the end of the placement, it is important to get up, shake your arms and legs, and walk around a bit.

The Marma points that are affected during the placement are 24, 25, 26, 36, and 37 (for a full explanation of the Marma points, see the appendix at the end of the book).

The symbols that increase the beneficial effect of this placement are number 1 – Cho-Ko-Rey, number 6 – Rakku, and number 12 – Ha-Loo.

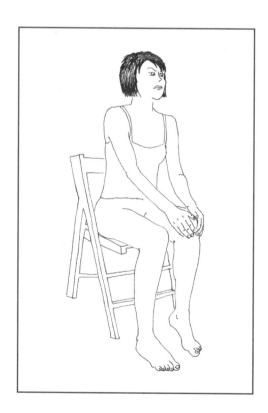

20 Holding the ankle – stability

Placement number 20 is the first of three "physical" positions whose objective is to treat your physical problems. This placement treats a lack of physical stability. The placement is performed sitting down, in a position that is comfortable for you. In the main, it involves holding your ankle in both hands – first the left ankle and then the right – for about three minutes, exerting gentle pressure. Master Naharo links this placement to the custom of washing feet. The placement releases pressure above the joints and improves stability.

There is no special meditation associated with this placement.

The Marma points that are affected during the placement are 28 and 29 (for a full explanation of the Marma points, see the appendix at the end of the book).

The symbols that increase the beneficial effect of this placement are number 3 – Hun-Sha-Zi-Shu-Neen, number 7 – Rakku-An, and number 11 – Har-Te.

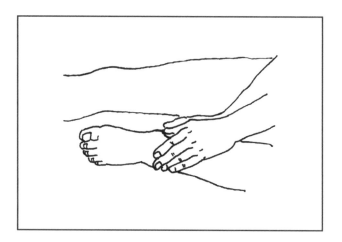

21 Holding the sole of the foot – contact (with the earth)

Similar to placement number 20, placement 21 is also "physical" and treats the problem of physical grounding to the earth. This placement is also performed sitting down. First you hold your left foot and then your right. Most of the holding of the foot is done in its center, one hand below and the other on the arch of the foot. The placement goes on for three minutes, with gentle pressure.

The Marma points that are affected during the placement are 30, 31, 32, and 33 (for a full explanation of the Marma points, see the appendix at the end of the book).

The symbols that increase the beneficial effect of this placement are number 2 – Se-He-Key, number 6 – Rakku, and number 9 – To-Ho.

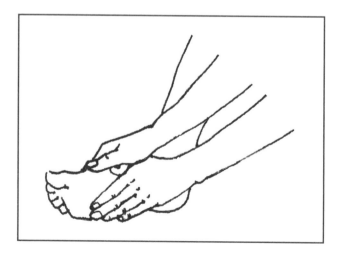

22 The back of the waist – rubbing

Placement number 22 is different than the other 21 placements, since it is a placement "in motion." The starting position is similar to that of number 17. After you have placed your hands on your body (slightly cupped), rub them on the posterior side of your body, down and up, with strong pressure. Master Naharo claims that this rubbing increases the action of the four lower chakras and causes Reiki energy to flow all over the body.

There is no time limit, nor is there a meditation directly associated with the placement.

There are no Marma points affected in any special way during the placement.

The symbols that increase the beneficial effect of this placement are number 4 are Di-Ko-Miyo, number 5 – Dai-Ku-Myo, and number 8 – Saa-Saa.

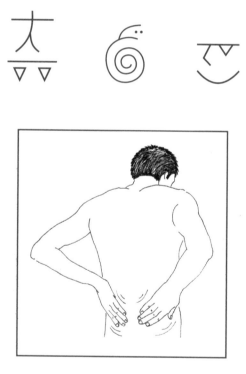

Some people claim that this placement is meant only for men (for self-treatment or for treating men). For this reason, we asked a male practitioner to demonstrate the placement. Master Naharo thinks that this placement is suitable for both sexes.

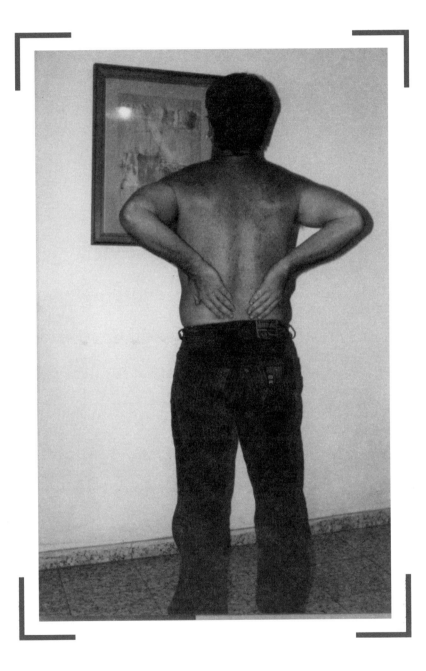

Applying the Hand Placements in Self-Treatment and in Treating Others

When Master Naharo determined the 22 basic hand placements in Reiki, he taught his senior pupils those placements and sent them all over the world to practice them on other people. (Gail Radford and Chantal Dupont were among the pupils who later collaborated in writing Reiki books, and Bill Waites wrote a basic Reiki book together with Master Naharo.) A year later, his pupils gathered in Poonah, and Master Naharo asked for their opinion.

It transpired that with regard to self-treatment, the pupils had observed the methods that the Master had propounded. The only changes were in the position of the body during the placement (standing, sitting, or lying on their back), and in the use of one or more of the three symbols that the Master had allocated for each placement. However, regarding the treatment of others, the pupils adopted a very wide range of placements that retained the underlying principle of the self-placement, but differed slightly from one another.

A few of the pupils were afraid that Master Naharo would reprimand them and demand that they employ a rigid, dogmatic method for treating others. To their surprise, the Master encouraged the variety. He told them: "Since you practice Reiki and are well-versed in transmitting it, you can do nothing bad. So long as you remember that the hand, straight or cupped, is the source of the Reiki that is transmitted, so long as you remember not to do to someone else what you do not want done to yourselves, every method is effective and correct."

It is possible to understand the problem by examining placement number 5 (capping the eyes) as an example. In self-treatment, this placement is natural and logical. However, what happens when it is applied to someone else? Let's suppose the recipient is lying on his back (most practitioners prefer to treat someone when he is lying on his back): the placement as it is in self-treatment would require that the practitioner straddle the recipient's body and lean close to it. That is not logical. Hand placement from the side would prevent the natural flow between the lines of the practitioner's hand and the fingers and the lines of the recipient's body. Therefore, quite naturally, a placement is chosen in which the practitioner stands behind the recipient and places his hands over the recipient's eyes with his fingers facing the recipient's feet (as opposed to facing the top of the head as in self-treatment). You can see the differences that occur by force of circumstance in the diagrams and photographs that follow.

Similar limitations and constraints exist in the positions of the body, on the back and on the legs of the recipient. In some cases, it is preferable to administer treatment from above (with the recipient located next to the practitioner's head), and in others, it is preferable to administer treatment from the side or from below (with the recipient located next to the practitioner's feet). So long as the rules of the hand placements are observed, every experienced practitioner – this generally means a pupil who has already qualified for or is studying toward Reiki II – can decide for himself his own treatment methods and placements. However, let us emphasize once again that in self-treatment, the pattern determined by Master Naharo must be observed.

Examples of applying self-treatment to the treatment of other people.

We now present a few examples of how it is possible to perform hand placements on other people, according to Master Naharo's Reiki principles, and change the self-applied hand placements.

Placement number 5 – Capping the eyes

Self-treatment

Treating another person

Placement number 6 – "Smacking" the cheeks (or in a similar way, 7 – pressing the temples)

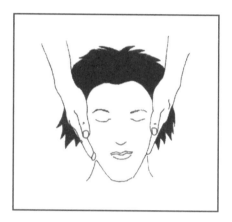

Self-treatment

Treating another person

A set of placements (for treating other people) number 12 (upper abdomen)

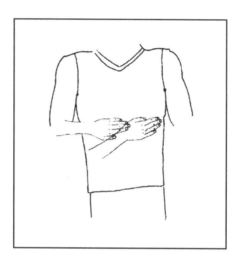

number 13 (lower abdomen)

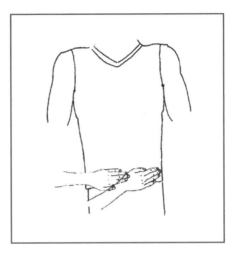

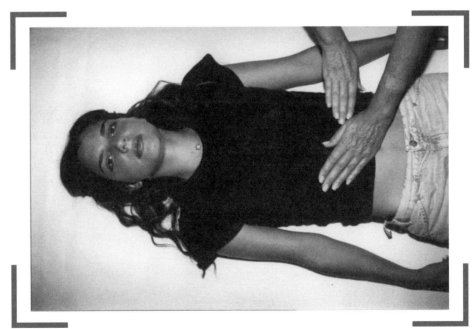

Treating another person

number 14 (thumb on the navel)

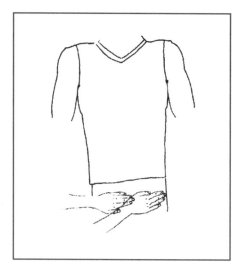

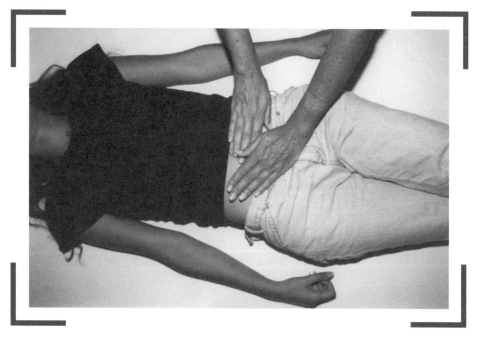

Treating another person

I will repeat a comment I made before. In a complete Reiki course, we are meticulous about teaching the correct method, that is, hand placements exactly as Master Naharo performs them. This is very important in self-treatment, and less important in the treatment of others. Having said that, it must be stressed that this is not an inflexible theory: if the practitioner feels that it is right for him to make slight changes in the hand placements or in the position of the arms or body (even to the point of switching arms), he must do it! In general, the practitioner makes sure that he performs the positions and placements in self-treatment correctly, and allows himself greater leeway when treating others.

Charging Reiki Energy

Whether for purposes of self-treatment or of treating other people or sending long-distance Reiki, a Reiki practitioner must go through the stage of "charging Reiki." This stage can be compared to charging a car battery – the motor is still, but it has all the potential to turn into an "energy machine." The person holding the keys does not yet feel the energy and does not exploit it, but he is well aware of the power in his hands. After a slight turn of the key, the situation changes – the motor suddenly becomes an "energy machine" and the person is conscious and controls the throbbing energy (at least we hope so). This is exactly what happens the moment we link up to Reiki energy.

When a practitioner wants to link up to Reiki energy, he must perform a simple process of hand positions, standing or sitting. (Even when the practitioner intends to administer self-treatment in a lying position, the initial link-up is still performed standing or sitting.)

1. The arms are bent at right angles, elbows close to the body, hands facing the ground, which is actually the source of Reiki.
2. The hands rise to a prayer position, touching each other and creating an "arrow" or "triangle" that points upward. While it is important that the fingers and thumbs touch each other, the points in the center of the palms, where the Reiki actually comes from, must be a hand's breadth apart.
3. The hands go down to their first position, with arms bent, elbows close to the body – and hands facing upward this time.

At this stage, the practitioner is in fact linked to the Reiki energy.

Many Reiki practitioners perform these three positions for charging Reiki before beginning every treatment (but not before every hand placement). One link-up like this is sufficient for a whole set of hand placements, and allows the practitioner to perform hand placements from each one of the three original positions.

At the end of the hand placement (the entire treatment), many Reiki practitioners tend to perform a symbolic "detachment" – they perform the three hand positions in the opposite order – 3, 2, 1.

Note that when the basic positions are performed, the Reiki symbols are not used.

4. The fourth position follows the performance of positions 1, 2, and 3 – that is, it is performed when the practitioner is already linked up to Reiki – and it is performed as if the practitioner were leaning on both hands (parallel to his body) on the wall, his hands facing away from him, and he sends the Reiki into the distance. This is in fact the position for sending long-distance Reiki. In this position, the Reiki symbols can be used.

Sending Long-Distance Reiki

The preferred Reiki treatment (self-treatment or treating others) is by actually placing the hands and making contact. The Reiki energy operates with the power of touch and the result is often astounding. However, it is not always possible to make actual contact, and we may still want to send Reiki to another person, or link someone who is far away from us (or a large group of people) up to Reiki energy.

Gradually, the Reiki practitioner will learn to send Reiki energy to others, and the distance between him and the other/s will not present an obstacle. (Master Naharo claims that it is possible to send Reiki energy into the future, but it is not possible to send Reiki energy into the past.) First, this ability will be expressed in sending Reiki to people who are close to the practitioner – in general, people to whom he has already transmitted Reiki in treatments that included touch. Over time, the practitioner will learn to send Reiki to people he does not know at all, to groups of people who need help (flood or earthquake victims, for example), and to various groups in society (sick people, for instance).

When sending long-distance Reiki, the stage when the practitioner links up to Reiki energy is important. It is important to perform the three basic positions (see pages 148–149), and then to go on to the fourth position, the position of "sending" Reiki. When he gets into that position, he must envision one of the Reiki symbols (he can also sketch it with his right index finger on his left palm). After that, there is the meditation stage in which the practitioner sees in his mind's eye the person or group to whom the Reiki energy is being sent. (There is no need to define the problem or the disease exactly – Reiki will find the blockage and effect the recovery by itself.)

"Sending" Reiki can be done over any distance. The process takes eight to fifteen minutes. When a group of practitioners gets together or sets a time to send Reiki to a particular person or group, Reiki energy is transmitted with unprecedented power – it is not merely 1 + 1 + 1 = 3... The Reiki energy that is sent is a thousand times more powerful than the sum total of the energy that passes through individuals practicing Reiki!

At the end of the process, the practitioner must break contact by going out of the meditation and performing the basic positions 3, 2, and 1.

Treating Animals and Plants

The principles of treating various animals or plants are amazingly simple, and in fact only require a slight modification on the part of the practitioner. In general, treating an animal requires only a little Reiki energy (regardless of the size of the animal), because animals absorb Reiki energy much better than humans do.

The practitioner performs Reiki "charging" – 1, 2, 3.

When the animal is small and can be held in one's hands, it is held in position 3 (hands facing upward), and Reiki is sent.

When the animal is large and can be touched, the hands are placed on it with the fingers facing its head.

When it is not possible to touch the animal because it is dangerous or far away from us, Reiki is sent in the same way as it is sent to people.

Treating plants is done by touch or by sending long-distance Reiki. During the touch, an effort must be made to ensure that the hands are placed in a way that the fingers are pointing at the top of the plant.

Treatment Sets

Over the course of time, traditional Reiki therapists adopt treatment sets that they use in their work. Such a set is actually a "sequence" of hand placements, each sequence consisting of between 3 and 8 hand placements. Master Naharo has added two "gates" to this – an entrance gate and an exit gate to the sequence. This gate is in fact a moment of meditation that is supported by one of the Reiki symbols. The entrance gate is performed before or together with the first placement, and the exit gate is performed together with or after the last placement.

We now present 20 different sets – two of them general (the contribution of Chantal Dupont to this book), which are used in all-over Reiki treatments, and 18 sets for treating various problems or blockages that are common among people.

Set 1 – treatment of a lack of self-confidence

Entrance gate: Symbol 4 – Di-Ko-Miyo

Placement 9

Placement 12

Placement 21

Placement 8

Exit gate: Symbol 10 – Zonar

Set 2 – treatment of headaches and migraines

Entrance gate: Symbol 7 – Rakku-An

Placement 1

Placement 10

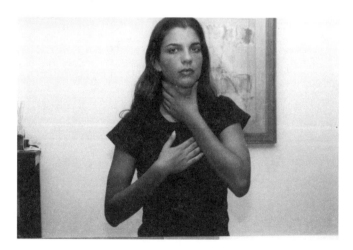

Placement 15

Placement 22

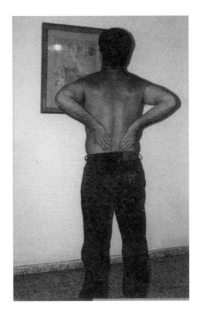

Placement 2

Exit gate: Symbol 11 – Har-Te

Set 3 – treatment of abdominal pains

Entrance gate: Symbol 8 – Saa-Saa

Placement 12

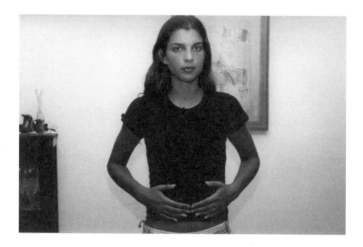

Placement 13

Placement 14

Placement 15

Exit gate: Symbol 5 – Dai-Ku-Myo

Set 4 – treatment of blockages in the blood and lymph systems

Entrance gate: Symbol 9 – To-Ho

Placement 5

Placement 10

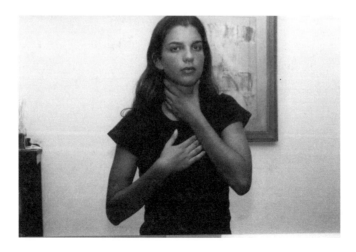

Placement 11

Placement 19

Placement 22

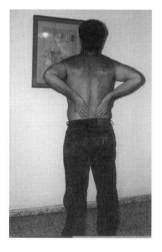

Exit gate: Symbol 12 – Ha-Loo

Set 5 – treatment of problems of impotence, infertility, and sexual blockages

Entrance gate: Symbol 2 – Se-He-Key

Placement 1

Placement 15

Placement 18

Placement 11

Placement 21

Exit gate: Symbol 6 – Rakku

Set 6 – general treatment of the anterior part of the body (according to Chantal Dupont)

Entrance gate: Symbol 1 – Cho-Ko-Rey

Placement 5

Placement 7

Placement 4

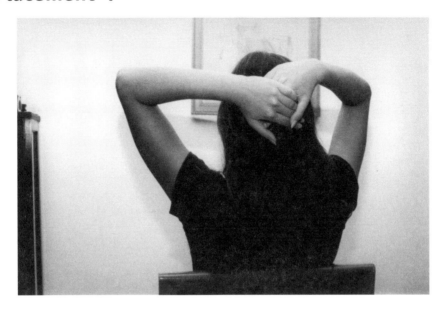

Placement 9

Placement 11

Placement 12

Placement 14

Placement 15

Exit gate: Symbol 3 – Hun-Sha-Ze-Shu-Neen

Set 6a – general treatment of the posterior part of the body (according to Chantal Dupont)

Entrance gate: Symbol 1 – Cho-Ko-Rey

Placement 8

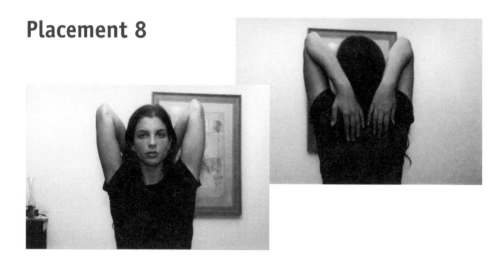

Placement 16

Placement 17

Placement 19

Exit gate: Symbol 3 – Hun-Sha-Ze-Shu-Neen

Set 7 – treatment of backaches

Entrance gate: Symbol 2 – Se-He-Key

Placement 8

Placement 16

Placement 17

Placement 22

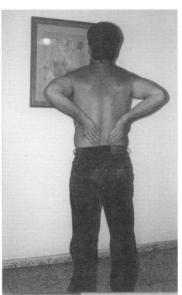

Placement 1

Exit gate: Symbol 10 – Zonar

Set 8 – treatment of mental depression

Entrance gate: Symbol 8 – Saa-Saa

Placement 2

Placement 3

Placement 6

Placement 12

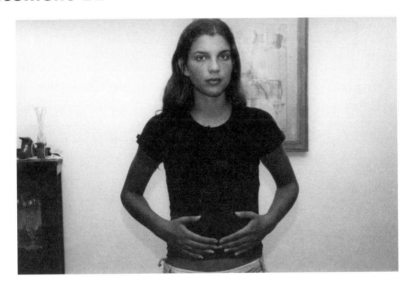

Exit gate: Symbol 4 – Di-Ko-Miyo

Set 9 – treatment of stress

Entrance gate: Symbol 9 – To-Ho

Placement 16

Placement 12

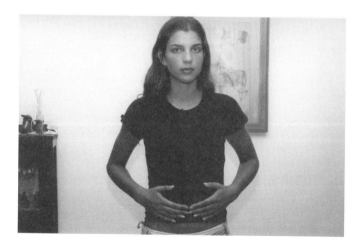

Placement 6

Placement 7

Exit gate: Symbol 11 – Har-Te

Set 10 – treatment of problems and blockages in the respiratory system

Entrance gate: Symbol 4 – Di-Ko-Miyo

Placement 21

Placement 9

Placement 11

Placement 12

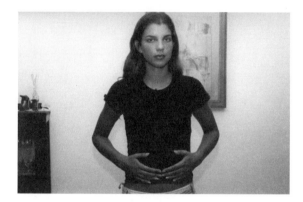

Placement 13

Exit gate: Symbol 12 – Ha-Loo

Set 11 – treatment of problems and blockages in the digestive system (including problems of nutrition, diet, and so on)

Entrance gate: Symbol 2 – Se-He-Key

Placement 12

Placement 20

Placement 18

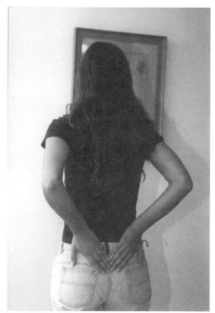

Exit gate: Symbol 9 – Saa-Saa

Set 12 – treatment of problems of a lack of energy, weakness, and so on

Entrance gate: Symbol 4 – Di-Ko-Miyo

Placement 2

Placement 3

Placement 7

Placement 19

Exit gate: Symbol 4 – Di-Ko-Miyo (identical to the entrance gate)

Set 13 – treatment of heart-related problems (including emotional problems of the heart)

Entrance gate: Symbol 9 – To-Hu

Placement 6

Placement 10

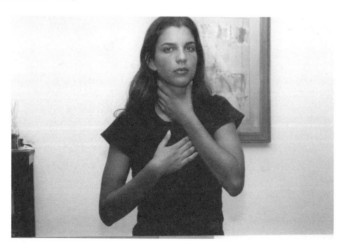

Placement 11

Placement 15

Placement 2

Exit gate: Symbol 10 – Zonar

Set 14 – treatment of problems of the excretory systems (urine, feces, perspiration, saliva)

Entrance gate: Symbol 7 – Rakku-An

Placement 4

Placement 22

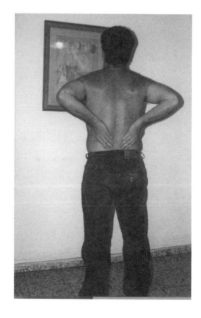

Placement 17

Placement 5

Placement 19

Exit gate: Symbol 8 – Saa-Saa

Set 15 – treatment of relationship problems

Entrance gate: Symbol 10 – Zonar

Placement 19

Placement 16

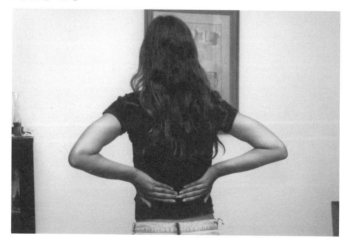

Placement 13

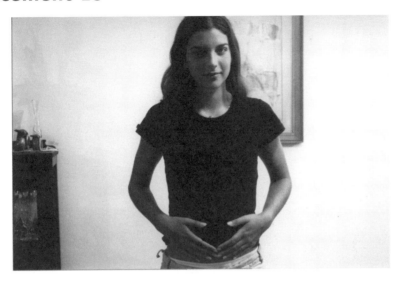

Placement 5

Exit gate: Symbol 11 – Har-Te

Set 16 – treatment of fear problems (phobias)

Entrance gate: Symbol 8 – Saa-Saa

Placement 21

Placement 18

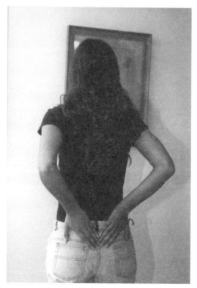

Placement 9

Placement 6

Exit gate: Symbol 10 – Zonar

Set 17 – treatment of psychosomatic problems

Entrance gate: Symbol 4 – Di-Ko-Miyo

Placement 18

Placement 14

Placement 10

Placement 5

Placement 4

Exit gate: Symbol 2 – Se-He-Key

Set 18 – treatment of concentration problems (inability to meditate) and poor memory

Entrance gate: Symbol 1 – Cho-Ko-Rey

Placement 5

Placement 8

Placement 17

Placement 19

Placement 22

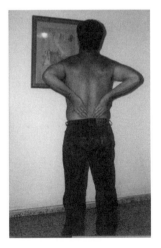

Exit gate: Symbol 12 – Ha-Loo

Set 19 – treatment of skeletal and joint pains (including toothache)

Entrance gate: Symbol 8 – Saa-Saa

Placement 4

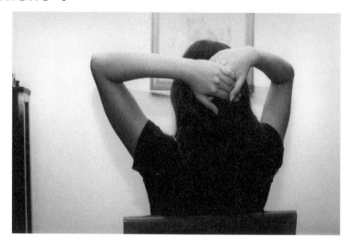

Placement 8

Placement 12

Placement 17

Placement 22

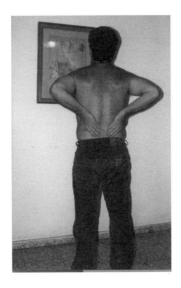

Exit gate: Symbol 6 – Rakku

Set 20 – treatment of hair problems (hair loss, balding, or hairiness)

Entrance gate: Symbol 9 – To-Hu

Placement 7

Placement 10

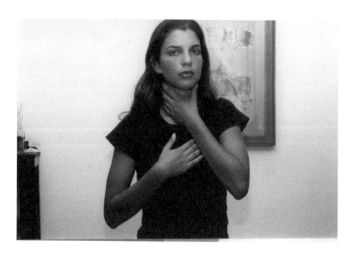

Placement 2

Placement 17

Exit gate: Symbol 1 – Cho-Ko-Rey

Reiki II Diploma

The Reiki II diploma is hereby awarded to

_____

upon learning and internalizing the Reiki principles, the Reiki symbols, and the hand placements.

This diploma qualifies _____
to receive the blessing of Reiki and to confer this blessing upon others by means of thought, and by means of treatment, in any manner he/she considers correct.

Master Naharo

Appendix

The Hidden Secrets of Reiki

To those interested in Reiki, it would seem that Reiki's secret lies in the symbols, the enigmatic signs passed first by means of initiation, from Master to student, emanating consciously from the teacher and absorbed unconsciously by the student.

Finally, in second-level Reiki, they are transmitted to the student in a conscious fashion. This, however, is not the hidden secret of Reiki.

The hidden secret of Reiki, the secret used by the experienced Reiki healer to treat almost everyone, whatever his affliction, is much more straightforward than this:

It is Marma.

Marma was defined by scholars of Chinese and Indian medicine in bygone days as points that provide the maximal contact between the physical body and the astral bodies which convey cosmic energy.

Marma points may be described as open channels, appearing in different locations in the body, where one opening is open to cosmic energy and another to the human body. Along the length of each channel are minute perforations that convey cosmic energy throughout the person's body – physical or ethereal.

The Marma points, about 52 in all, form the basis of the entire meridian network and all the acupuncture/pressure/massage points used in alternative medicine.

However, the ability of the Reiki expert to make the most of these points is far greater than in any other technique; he opens the connecting channel, and the Reiki energy flows through into the correct place, in the right quantity and potency, healing the body and mind in the particular area 'controlled' by the Marma point.

Many Reiki teachers are displeased that I am divulging this valuable information to anyone who reads this book.

I actually did deliberate a great deal about this issue, but finally the orders of my esteemed teacher, who taught me the Marma points and instructed me to disseminate the knowledge, overcame my reluctance:

"Reiki is everyone's property and no one has the right to keep the information to himself," he instructed me.

I therefore offer the full list of Marma points, describing their location in the body, the English transliteration of their Sanskrit names (I learned these names in India), and the area controlled by the point.

Remember that there is pairing and parallelism between the body's Marma points: A point on the right arm has an equivalent point on the left arm. A point appearing on one side of the spinal column will appear on the other side, in the identical position and at the same distance from the spine.

1. The point located between the lower and middle thumb phalanges, at the junction of the thumb with the palm, is the Kshipra point. It controls passion and spiritual will power during the day, and the stomach, on the physical level, during the night.
2. The point on the palm of the hand, on the mound located beneath the pinkie, is the Kshiprai point. It controls passion and spiritual will power during the night, and the stomach, on the physical level, during the day.
3. The point found precisely in the center of the palm, that is, two points, one at the center of the palm of each hand, is the Talhridaya point, which is directly connected to the heart.
4. Five points, one at the end of each finger (ten points in all for both hands), are referred to as a single point. These are known as the Talhridayass points and are linked to the nervous system.

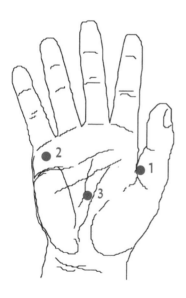
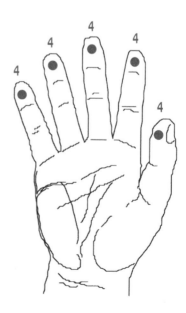

5. The point found on the joint of the hand, beneath the thumb, at the place where the pulse is measured, is known as Manibandha. It is most important since it indicates an individual's capacity to express and make the most of his potential in the world. It is the main spiritual indicator in every Reiki treatment.

6. The point found on the hand joint, parallel to point 5 but beneath the pinkie, is called Koorchsha and is responsible for blood circulation.

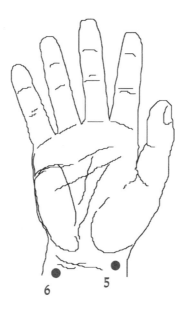

7. The point found on the arm, in the inner crease of the elbow joint, is known as Karpooram and is the main point connected to vitality and sexual energy.

8. Two points (on each arm), located on either side of the elbow, are known as Kurpara and are responsible for the liver, the urinary tract and the pancreas.

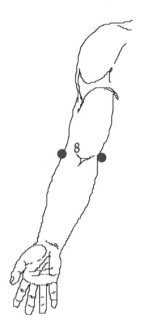

9. The point found on the outside of the arm, halfway between the elbow and the shoulder, is known as Oorvi and is responsible for the blood flow rate.

10. Two points at the back of the neck, separated by the two finger-widths (of the particular person), are called Kraknrik and are responsible for the heart chakra (opening and closing), the lungs and the chest. These are important points in every Reiki treatment.

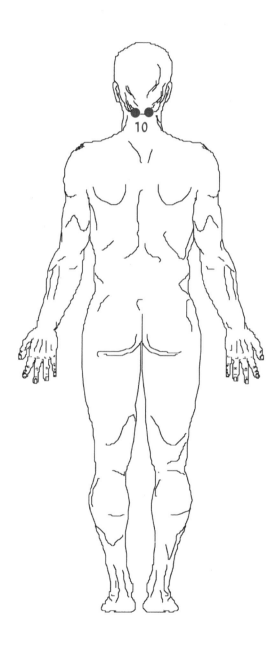

11. One point located in the center of the skull, at the back, facing the third eye chakra, is known as the upper Kraknrik. It is an important point, responsible for allergies, depression and low spirits, which some ignore due to the difficulty in treating it.

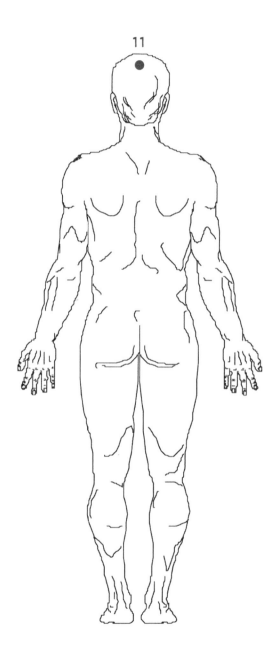

12. Two points situated on the neck, at the front, under the ears, are the well known Manya, which are responsible for the blood capillaries and blood flow through the secondary blood vessels (that is, not veins and arteries).
13. Two points at the base of the neck are the well known Shamantrika, points which are responsible for the main blood vessels – the aorta, arteries and veins.
14. One point located at the bottom of the lower triangle of the neck, between the bones is the important Neela point, which is responsible for the fifth chakra and the thyroid gland.

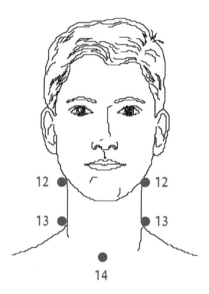

15. One point (it has no parallel on the opposite side of the body) in the upper left section of the chest, beneath the lateral bone, in a straight line down from the left ear, is the Apastamgh point. This is connected to muscle action, including that of the heart, and is treated in cases of muscle tension.

16. One point exactly parallel to point number 15, but on the right side of the chest is the important Kakshadhara point. This is also associated with muscular activity, including that of the heart, treated in cases of muscle slackness.

17. One point located exactly in the center of the chest, on the line connecting the armpits, is the Hridayam point, responsible for the fourth chakra and the thymus gland.

18. One point located a finger-width below point 17, is the lower Hridayam point which is directly connected to the heart.

19. One point located five finger-widths below point 18 is the well-known Manipura point which is in charge of the third chakra and human will power.

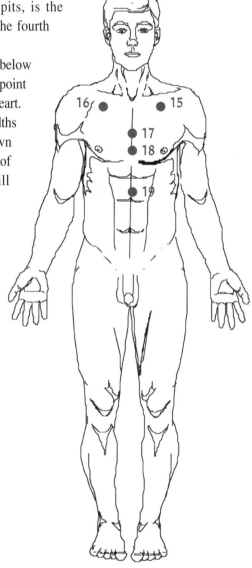

20. One central point located beneath the navel, three finger-widths below, is the Nabi point. This is one of the most important points in Reiki and is responsible for the second chakra (sexual), physical and emotional equilibrium, human creativity, judgment, and drawing conclusions.

21. One point located above the groin is known as Vasth. It is the main point for everything concerning sexual ability, in the sense of fertility and fertilization and ability to reproduce, and is a very important point in Reiki.

22. One point located in the center of the groin (in men a little more to the left) is known as Lohitaksham. This point is responsible for the lymphatic system.

23. The point located in the center of the front of the thigh (in both thighs) is known as Oovi and is responsible for walking (and in the spiritual sense, for an individual to advance toward his/her goals).

24. The point located three finger-widths above the knee, known as Ani, is responsible for balance.

25. Two points (on each knee), one exactly above the center front of the knee, the other parallel to it on the inside of the knee, are the upper Janu points. They are responsible for balance (both physical and spiritual).

26. Two points (on each knee), one exactly below the center front of the knee, the other parallel to it on the inside of the knee, are the lower Janu points and are responsible for the joints in the body.

27. The point in the center of the shin, halfway between the knee and the ankle, is the Januara point and is responsible for the kidneys and the flow of adrenaline in the body.

28. The point located on the inner side of the shin, seven finger-widths from the ankle, is known as the upper Gulpha point, and is an important point in the male reproductive system.

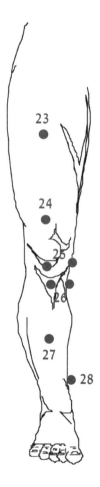

29. Two points located on the ankle, one at the front, the second on the inner side, are the lower Gulpha points, responsible for the female reproductive system.
(Note that in Reiki, points 28 and 29 are treated jointly for both male and female reproductive problems).
30. Five points, located at the junctions of the toes with the foot, are the Khipram points, responsible for the sinuses and to some extent the lymphatic system.

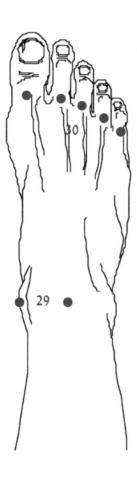

31. The point located on the sole of the foot, in the middle of the mound beneath the big toe, is known as Koorcha, and is responsible for the stomach. It is an important point in Reiki and a central point in reflexology.
32. The point located on the sole of the foot, in the groove in the center of the foot, is known as Talhridayam and is directly connected to the heart.
33. The point located on the sole of the foot, in the center of the ankle, is the famous Koorchshir point, which is responsible for the first chakra.

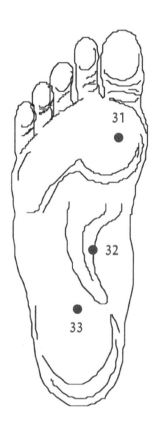

34. The point located at the center of the shin, at the back, eight finger-widths from the ankle, is the lower Indravastih point. It is responsible for athletic ability (the ability to operate muscles rapidly and with full power).
35. The point located five finger-widths above point 34, at the center of the shin at the back, is the upper Indravastih point. It is responsible for muscle contraction (or pain in the limbs, mostly the feet).
36. The point located behind the knee, at the center, is called Janu and is an extremely important point. It controls the function of the liver, the urinary tract and the spleen, and is a central point in every Reiki treatment.
37. The point located at the back of the thigh, five finger-widths above the knee crease, is the well known Aanih point and is linked to the genital organs.
38. The point located at the upper back of the thigh, two finger-widths below the junction of the buttock and thigh, is the Vorvee point, which deals particularly with blood circulation in the legs.

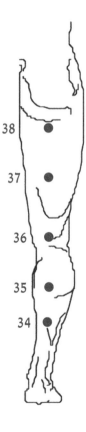

39. Two points located in the center of the buttocks, known as Kteektaninam, are key points in achieving physical, emotional and spiritual equilibrium (including sense of balance). They are an important part of any Reiki treatment.

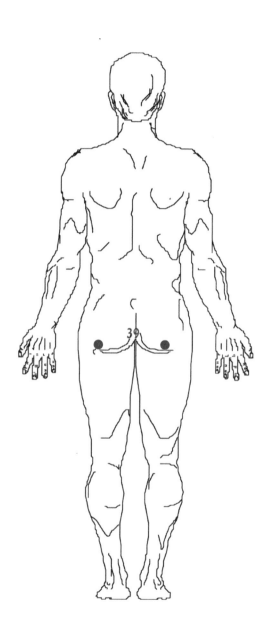

40. One point located in the upper zone of the ridge between the buttocks, where a small hollow can be felt, is the famous Gudam point, which is directly linked to the first chakra.

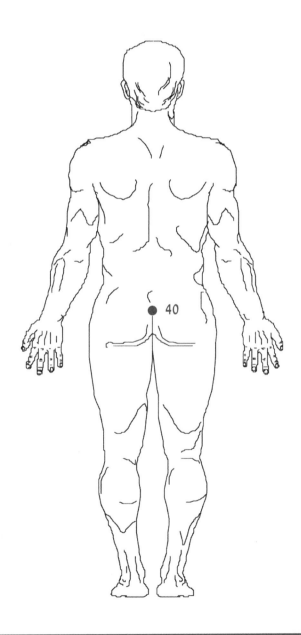

41. Two points located five finger-widths above point 40 and two finger-widths from the spine (in each direction) are the Kukundaraye points, which are linked to the second chakra.

42. Two points located five finger-widths above point 41, and four finger-widths from the spine in each direction, are the Nitamba points. They are associated with kidney function.

43. Two points located five finger-widths above point 42, the same distance from the spine as in point 42, are the Koopram points. They are responsible for adrenaline balance in the body.

44. Two points on the lower section of the shoulder-blades, four finger-widths from the spine, are the Vrahti points, associated with the heart and lungs.

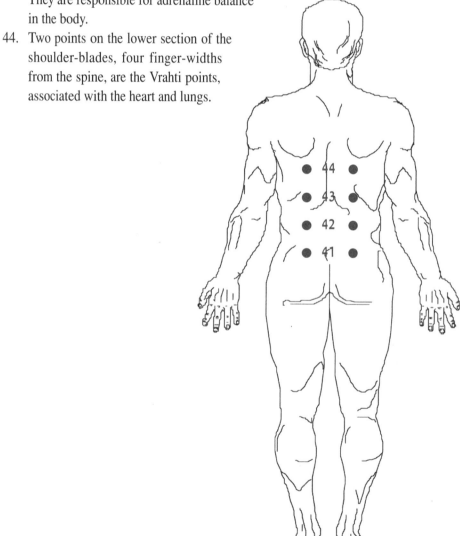

45. Two points located on the upper section of the shoulder-blades, above point 44, are the Asphalakah, associated with the thymus gland and the heart.

46. The point located at the top edge of the shoulder, about a finger-width from the end, is the famous Asaha point, associated with the nervous system.

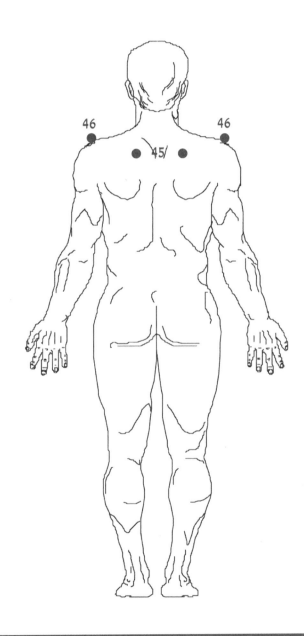

47. The point located above the ear, toward the eye (at the temple) on the skull, is the Shaunkh point, associated with hearing (not only in the physical sense, but also in the spiritual sense).

48. A point located above the ear toward the back of the neck ("shadow of the ear") on the skull, is the Utkshepau point that regulates brain function and is important in any state of increased awareness or enlightenment.

49. The point located at the center of the temple, known as the Apa, is directly linked to sight, not just in the physical sense but primarily in the spiritual sense. It is important in all Reiki treatment.

50. The point located in the middle of the brow (above the hair line), is the Sthapui, which is linked to the fifth chakra.

51. The point located at the center of the top of the skull, at the junction of the skull bones (where the fontanelle is visible in a baby's skull), is the Adhipati, which balances the seventh chakra and is very important in developing an individual's spiritual awareness.

52. The point at the center of the back of the head, on top, before the downward slope of the skull begins, is the Nadi, which is responsible for posture.

Note that the 52 points can overlap. This means, therefore, that an organ, system or problem of a medical/spiritual nature may be treated using different treatment positions (with the patient lying on his back or stomach, and so on).

If you are inexperienced in using Marma points, I recommend placing the entire palm of your hand on the point you wish to treat and transmitting the Reiki in this fashion. If you are experienced, the most effective treatment is to place the cushion of the thumb on the desired point. When there are two points, use both thumbs. When there is only one point, put your thumbs together on the point and direct the Reiki towards it.

This list is taken from *Reiki – A Practical Guide*, by Bill Waites and Master Naharo (Astrolog, 1998).

The Chakras

Many ancient civilizations relate to energy centers through which energy passes, entering and leaving and changing the body's energy field. According to the Hopi tribe in North America, the human body is built according to the same principles as the earth. Both the earth and human beings have an axis. The earth's north-south polar axis parallels the spinal column, the north pole parallels the brain, and the south pole parallels the base of the spinal column – the coccyx. The spinal column is responsible for the body's equilibrium. Not only are the nerve centers located along this axis, but so are the energy centers. The centers are responsible for the person's physical, mental, and spiritual functions.

Oriental medicine relates in depth to the significance of the etheric body and the energy centers in human beings. The Indians call these centers "chakras." The word "chakra" means "wheel." Every chakra manifests itself in the physical body, mainly in one of the endocrine glands that regulate all the physical and mental processes of the human body. Higher – cosmic – energies are channeled through the chakras to the physical and other human bodies. This energy, which is also called life energy, flows through the chakras, and is of cardinal importance for our lives and for our physical, mental, and spiritual health. When a situation arises in which the energy does not flow through the chakras in a harmonious manner, or when one of the chakras is either blocked or open too wide, an imbalance occurs, and this is evident in every aspect of life. The state of imbalance in the chakra will affect the endocrine gland to which the chakra is linked, and the body's delicate metabolic balance will be upset.

Each of the aura layers mentioned in the previous chapter, in addition to the material body – as well as everything else that exists in the universe – has its own unique vibrational frequency. In human beings, all the aura layers are supposed to be harmoniously joined and linked. If one of the aura layers is not linked to the others, the passage of information and energy between the bodies is disrupted.

For instance, when there is a rift between the mental (thought) body and the emotional body, a situation in which the person is unable to express his thoughts is liable to occur. Another rift causes a situation in which the person is unable to translate his emotions and thoughts into creation or action; and so on.

Like every other sophisticated "appliance" that works according to the principle of giving and taking (receiving and transmitting), human beings also require centers for receiving, transmitting, and converting energy. These centers are the chakras. In the physical body, the chakras function as "transmitters." They transmit the currents that arrive from the higher, more refined energy, which operates on higher frequencies of energetic bodies, to the physical body, while "converting" the frequency to one that our physical body can use.

In the same way that domestic use of electrical energy at a different frequency can cause a short-circuit, so it is if the energy that operates at higher frequencies is not converted in human beings. We can compare the action of the human body to the way in which we use electricity. We get our electrical energy from a source that contains enormously powerful electricity (the Electric Company). Electrical energy is conveyed to private homes by means of cables that carry electricity in appropriate and correct quantities, and not more. If too powerful an electric current were to be conveyed to a home, the results would be disastrous. On the other hand, plants and factories that require a large amount of electricity, and have a suitable infrastructure, receive and consume a much larger amount of electricity than private homes.

The aura layer that absorbs and contains the person's breath of life within it is the spiritual body, which is our divine side, and links us to creation. From this link, the energy passes to the other aura layers, each of which has a different purpose and vocation, and for that reason, requires a different quality of energy at a different frequency.

On each level, there are stations that convert the energy into a form that is suitable for the next level.

The entire universe is linked by a tremendous, primeval force. This force is transferred to every thing and every creature, according to their capacity, and in accordance with the frequencies that are compatible with them from the physiological, emotion, intellectual, and spiritual points of view. When the energy makes its way from this tremendous, primeval force to the bodies in the universe, its power and strength seem to decrease more and more, so that these bodies can absorb it, since they cannot cope with even one particle of the "non-decreased" power.

The human body, like the universe, consists of different strata – a spiritual stratum, an emotional stratum, and an intellectual stratum. The difference between the human body and the "body" of the cosmos lies solely in their wavelengths and frequencies. For that reason, the divine force is found not only outside of us, but also inside us. Since human beings have the ability to use the gift of the imagination, they can tune themselves intellectually, intuitively, or emotionally into the various energy bodies and strata of awareness, and change them.

Every method that broadens awareness, such as positive thinking, directed imagining, meditation, and many others, helps people tune themselves.

The chakras and awareness

Our awareness is our strongest tool as human beings. Our awareness can move about in our multidimensional being via the different strata. These changes – which are, in fact, the movement – may occur regularly and quickly. For this reason, the energy centers of the body are extremely important. Every chakra serves as a relay and transmitting station to a particular zone of frequency or awareness. When attention is focused on one of the chakras, the person is consciously or unconsciously involved mainly with the areas for which that chakra is "responsible."

With the help of their spiritual abilities, the sages of ancient China and India received information about the human energy system. They wrote this information down in vedas, which contain the ancient knowledge.

In India, as in other ancient and enlightened civilizations, the chakras are linked to particular colors, elements, symbols, and characteristics. The combination of these factors, which are linked to a certain chakra – for instance, during the chanting of a mantra that is attributed to that chakra, while looking at a certain shape or a certain color – creates a certain frequency that may link up, at a certain resonance, to a certain element in the human body. For example, the earth element is linked to the sex glands, to the first chakra, to the planet Mars, to the color red, to the ruby... and so on. This technique affords general equilibrium, which affects the person as well as the factors that are involved in the process.

This action also works in the opposite direction. When the person concentrates on a certain characteristic, wish, or ambition, allows them to dominate his life, and lives according to them, a situation is created whereby he works, lives, and communicates more from within the chakra that is linked to the area to which he attributes extreme importance. This is again a situation of "What came first – the chicken or the egg?" in which a certain perception, way of thinking, and form of behavior lead to an imbalance in the chakras. This imbalance is liable to exacerbate the situation enormously. It is difficult to say whether the imbalance in the chakras is what caused the behavioral, thought, and emotional imbalance, or vice versa.

Let's take a look at a common example of this imbalance. A person's sole interest is in increasing his income, and amassing more and more money and property. He spends most of his time concentrating on mundane problems and material and physical matters, and pays no attention to intellectual, mental, or spiritual development at a higher level. This person's awareness is focused significantly on the first chakra, and most of his thoughts concern survival, income, and material issues. But even when most of the person's focus of interest is linked to a particular chakra – in an unbalanced manner – it is liable to manifest itself in a number of ways. For example, excessive concentration on the first chakra may characterize a person with violent impulses, and a lust for mammon or sex –

or, on the other hand, this strong energy may be characterized by a powerful life force and a high degree of vitality. So, even concentration on a particular chakra – which ultimately creates some kind of imbalance – is likely to be expressed in many different forms, according to the development of the individual personality.

In the same way, the chakra's colors, as they are manifested in the aura, may also change. In the above example, the color of the first, or base, chakra, may appear in different shades of red, ranging from dark, "dirty" red, which indicates extreme materialistic behavior, or even addiction to drugs or alcohol, to light, "clean" red, which may attest to a sensitive person who copes with his surroundings well, but is also very interested in material matters. This situation may occur in the other chakras, and, of course, will be expressed in the colors of the entire aura.

The more a person concentrates and focuses on one area of life and awareness – such as creativity, materialism, mental development, spiritual development, and so on – the more obvious this fact will be in the action of the chakra that is responsible for this area. Because of the interrelationship among the chakras, it affects the state of the other chakras, all the person's realms of awareness and being, and his aura layers.

When a strong frequency of a particular color – yellow, for instance – is seen in the aura, it means that most of the person's awareness is concentrated on the "yellow" chakra – the third or solar plexus chakra. This may be an indication of a sensitive stomach, and a situation in which the third chakra is open or opens at the time. On the other hand, it can indicate a greater amount of concentration on the action of the third chakra – for example, the desire to be freer, or totally independent. These desires, which lead to focusing on the action of the third chakra, radiate onto the entire aura, and turn yellow into the dominant color at that time.

The aura layers are linked to the aura, to the electromagnetic field, by means of the chakras.

According to the colors of the person's aura, it is possible to know if his awareness is based more in the physical, mental, spiritual, or intellectual stratum, and if there is a certain imbalance between these areas and the action of the chakras.

The significance of the chakras

As we explained earlier, every chakra is linked to a particular color, sense, sound, element, endocrine gland, symbol, crystal, and body, as well as certain physical, mental, and spiritual characteristics.

There are numerous energy centers – like chakras – in the human body. In various ancient systems, more than seven major chakras are described. (In the Kabbalah, for instance, the "spheres," of which there are ten, parallel the chakras; in certain Oriental systems, 13 centers are mentioned; and so on.) However, here we will focus on the seven major chakras that are the best known and the most widely accepted.

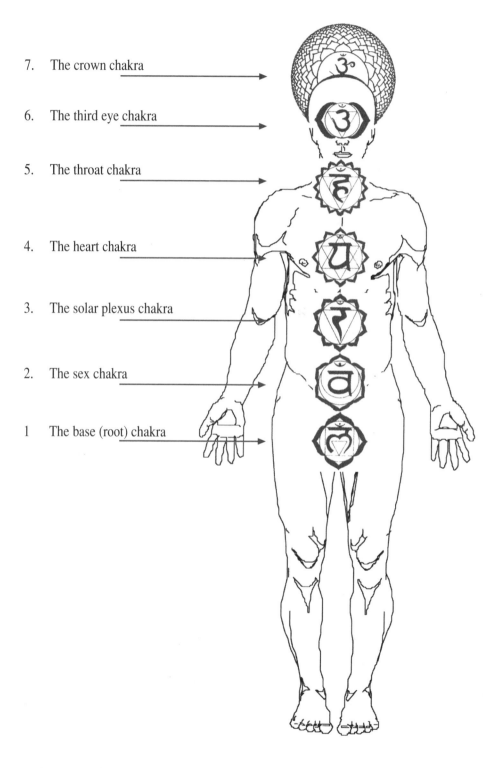

7. The crown chakra

6. The third eye chakra

5. The throat chakra

4. The heart chakra

3. The solar plexus chakra

2. The sex chakra

1   The base (root) chakra

The first chakra – the Base (Root) Chakra

This chakra symbolizes the struggle to survive, the basic needs, the ability to be assertive, and the link to the earth. It is also called the Root Chakra, and its Indian name is Muladhara, which means "base" or "root." The chakra is located between the anus and the genitals. Its colors are black and red. (Black does not appear in the aura's colors, but it is possible to balance the chakra by means of certain black stones, and therefore black is also one of its colors.) According to ancient Indian writings, the sense that is linked to this chakra is the sense of smell, and the sound that is linked to it, according to those writings, is "lam."

In the Indian tradition, the sign or symbol that relates to this chakra is a circle surrounded by four lotus leaves, with a square inside it, sometimes in yellow-gold, symbolizing the material world, and containing the letters of the sound "lam." A kind of "pipe" emerges from it, symbolizing the link of the chakra to the rest of the chakras and to the universal force that fills it with energy. The element that is linked to this chakra is earth, and the endocrine glands that are linked to it are the sex glands.

The organs linked to this chakra are the spinal column and the skeleton, the excretory organs, and the reproductive and physical continuity organs.

This chakra is linked to the person's basic survival instinct, to existential fears, to his ability to be practical and to function successfully in the material world, to the ability to have both feet firmly on the ground, and to make decisions. It links spiritual ability and the physical expression of this ability. When the chakra is in a state of harmonious action, it is expressed in powerful sexuality, being energetic and active, strong vitality, stability, and the ability to discern. An imbalance in the chakra is expressed in sexual promiscuity, sexual imbalance, deep anxiety, aggressiveness, disproportional focus on money and material things, lust for sex and mammon, lack of confidence, instability, detachment, delusion, and strong egocentricity.

From the physical point of view, an imbalance in this chakra is liable to be expressed in infertility, venereal diseases or diseases associated with sexuality, hemorrhoids, constipation, and problems in the skeleton and joints.

Exercises for balancing the chakra

The second chakra – the Sex Chakra

This chakra symbolizes emotions, sexuality, and sensuality. Its Indian name is Svadhisthana, which means "inside the body." The chakra is located on the pelvis, between the pubic bones. Its color is mainly orange, but also yellow that tends to orange. According to ancient Indian writings, the sense that is linked to this chakra is the sense of taste, and the sound that is linked to it, according to those writings, is "vam."

The sign that relates to this chakra is a circle surrounded by five lotus leaves, with a circle inside it (usually red), symbolizing and containing the letters of the sound "vam." A kind of "pipe" emerges from it, symbolizing the link of the chakra to the rest of the chakras and to the universal force. Sometimes a silver-gray crescent appears inside the circle. The element that is linked to this chakra is water, and the endocrine gland that is linked to it is the adrenal gland.

The organs linked to this chakra are the blood and the lymph, the digestive juices, the kidneys, the bladder, the muscles, and the sex organs.

This chakra symbolizes change and individuality, while understanding the uniqueness of other people. It is linked to enjoyment, sexuality, the desire to procreate, self-satisfaction, creativity, self-realization, and devotion to one's personal path. When the chakra is not balanced, this is expressed in many unrequited passions, which the person tries to realize in all kinds of ways (such as addiction to sex or food, and so on), a tendency to be jealous, restlessness, a lack of sexual balance, and problems in creating social and conjugal ties (problems that lead to loneliness).

From the physical point of view, a state of disharmony in the chakra is expressed in unbalanced circulation, kidney and gallbladder problems, frigidity, impotence, and muscular problems.

Exercise for balancing the chakra

The third chakra – the Solar Plexus Chakra

This chakra symbolizes the development of the personality, the ability to influence, power, and the practical facet of the intellect. The Indian name of this chakra is Manipura, which means "the palace of the diamond." The chakra is located on the solar plexus, in the region of the diaphragm. Its color is mainly yellow, but also blue. According to ancient Indian writings, the sense that is linked to this chakra is the sense of sight, and the sound that is linked to it, according to Indian tradition, is "ram."

The sign that relates to this chakra is a circle surrounded by ten lotus leaves, with a triangle inside it (usually red), containing the letters of the sound "ram." A kind of "pipe" emerges from it, symbolizing the link of the chakra to the rest of the chakras and to the universal force. The element that is linked to this chakra is fire, and the endocrine gland that is linked to it is the pancreas.

The organs linked to this chakra are the respiratory system and the diaphragm, the digestive system, the stomach, the pancreas, the liver, the spleen, the gallbladder, the small intestine, the extra-renal glands, and the sympathetic nervous system.

This chakra represents the ego; it is the source of all feelings and emotions, deeds, strength, self-will, the I, and realizing the I. Through this chakra, the person links up to the outside world and interprets it according to the balance of the chakra. When the chakra is in a state of balance, the person is courageous, creative, independent, tolerant, and strong in personality. An imbalance in the chakra is expressed in an unbalanced ego, dependence, manipulative behavior, exploitation of power, domineering behavior, arrogance, and fears.

From the physical point of view, an imbalance in this chakra is expressed in the physical body as problems in the liver, the gallbladder, and the eyes.

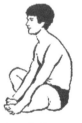

Exercises for balancing the chakra

The fourth chakra – the Heart Chakra

This chakra symbolizes love, caring, devotion, the ability to cure and heal, giving, and a lack of selfishness. Its Indian name is Anahata, which means "the ever-beating drum." The chakra is located in the center of the chest, parallel to the heart, and it links the upper chakras to the lower ones. Its colors are pink and green. According to Indian tradition, the sense that is linked to this chakra is the sense of touch, and the sound that is linked to it, according to ancient Indian writings, is "yam."

The sign or symbol that relates to this chakra is a circle surrounded by twelve lotus leaves, with a six-pointed star inside it, containing the letters of the sound "yam." A kind of "pipe" emerges from it, symbolizing the link of the chakra to the rest of the chakras and to the universal force. An additional symbolic element associated with this chakra is gray-green smoke. The element that is linked to this chakra is air, and the endocrine gland that is linked to it is the thymus gland.

The organs linked to this chakra are the heart, the circulatory system, the lungs, the immune system, the thymus gland, the skin, and the hands.

This chakra is linked to the ability to love, the ability to give and receive love unconditionally, forgiveness, compassion, generosity of heart and pocket, unselfishness, and the will and ability to give to others. It links spiritual ability and the physical expression of this ability. If the chakra is in a state of disharmony, it is expressed in selfishness, an inability to give and receive love, fears and anxieties, lust for mammon, stinginess, hesitancy, and indecisiveness.

Because this chakra links the lower chakras with the upper ones, when this chakra is blocked, the effects of the blockage are felt in the entire body.

From the physical point of view, an imbalance in this chakra is liable to be expressed in asthma, and circulatory, respiratory, and cardiac problems.

Exercise for balancing the chakra

The fifth chakra – the Throat Chakra

This chakra symbolizes creativity, the ability to express oneself, communication, and inspiration. Its Indian name is Visuddha, which means "full of purity." The chakra is located in the throat. Its colors are blue and light-blue. According to Indian tradition, the sense that is linked to this chakra is the sense of hearing.

The sign that relates to this chakra is a circle surrounded by sixteen lotus leaves, with a circle inside it, or a circle with a triangle inside it. A kind of "pipe" emerges from it, containing the letters of the sound "ham." The element that is linked to this chakra is blue sky, and the endocrine gland that is linked to it is the thyroid gland.

The organs linked to this chakra are the throat, the neck, the vocal cords, the vocal organs, the thyroid gland, the nerves, the ears, and the muscles.

This chakra is linked to all aspects of communication, the ability to communicate well, harmony with one's surroundings, the ability to express oneself, creativity, self-image, and faith. It links thought to the expression of thought. If the chakra is in a state of disharmony, it is expressed in communication problems, the inability to express thoughts and desires, a lack of creativity, anger, apathy, indifference, and conflicts between emotion and logic.

From the physical point of view, an imbalance in this chakra is expressed in inflammations, infections, and vocal problems.

Exercise for balancing the chakra

The sixth chakra – the Third Eye Chakra

This chakra symbolizes intuition, intellectual power, will power, and knowledge. Its Indian name is Ajna, which means "command center." The chakra is located on the forehead, between the eyebrows. Its colors are purple and indigo. According to Indian tradition, the sense that is linked to this chakra is the intuition (the sixth sense), and the sound that is linked to it is "kasham."

The sign that relates to this chakra is a sky-blue circle surrounded on both sides by large lotus leaves, with a drawing of two feet inside it. A kind of "pipe" emerges from it, containing the letters of the sound "kasham." The element that is linked to this chakra is ether, and the endocrine gland that is linked to it is the pituitary gland, which is responsible for the action of all the endocrine glands and all hormonal action.

The organs linked to this chakra are the various parts of the brain, the central nervous system, the face, the eyes, the ears, and the nose.

This chakra is the one that links the person to his subconscious, intuition, the ability to comprehend cosmic insights and to receive non-verbal messages. It is responsible for balancing the two cerebral hemispheres, left and right, that is, intuition and emotion (and mysticism) with logic and reason. It is also responsible for physical balance, the ability to concentrate, peace of mind, wisdom, and extra-sensory perception. When the chakra is balanced, the person will have the qualities of popularity, powerful intuition, high morality, and clarity. If the chakra is in a state of imbalance, it is expressed in depression, dependence, unrequited passions, indecisiveness, imbalance, mental exhaustion, auditory and visual problems, and learning and comprehension problems.

From the physical point of view, an imbalance in this chakra is liable to be expressed in headaches, nightmares, nerve problems, and ear and eye problems.

Exercises for balancing the chakra

The seventh chakra – the Crown Chakra

This chakra symbolizes enlightenment, knowledge, and linking up to the higher strata of spiritual awareness. Its Indian name is Sasharata, which means "the lotus flower with a thousand petals." The chakra is located on the crown of the head. Its colors are purple and white. The sense that is linked to this chakra is the finest and most delicate sense that constitutes the ability to tune oneself in to supreme messages and the universal force (which perhaps can be called "the sense of enlightenment"). The sound that is linked to it is "om."

The sign that relates to this chakra is a lotus with a thousand petals with the letters of the sound "om" above it. The element that is linked to this chakra is the ether and space element, and the endocrine gland that is linked to it is the pineal gland.

The organ linked to this chakra is the brain.

This chakra is responsible for linking up to higher awareness, the ability to receive divine and cosmic insights, and the ability to link up to divine knowledge and the light of universal love. When the chakra is open and balanced, the person is blessed with enlightenment, and enjoys a harmonious and satisfying life. If the chakra is in a state of imbalance, it is liable to be expressed in boredom, a lack of purpose, the inability to open up to spiritual dimensions, the lack of perfect awareness, extreme situations, and situations of coma and death.

Exercises for balancing the chakra

[This chapter is taken from *Color Healing – A Practical Guide*, by Graham Travis (Astrolog, 2000).]

Meditation

This brief appendix does not serve as a substitute for an in-depth discussion on meditation. Its sole purpose is to present one general meditation, which can teach about the others.

Meditation involves focusing on one's inner self, creating a bridge between one's consciousness and one's inner world, the subconscious… thus also creating an easier link with the universe, with pure universal energy, and with the extrasensory world.

Meditation requires three components:

1. The person's decision to meditate.
2. Suitable surroundings for meditating.
3. Familiarity with and ability to control bodily systems, especially the respiratory system.

For example, we will present a short meditation exercise, which is mainly effective in dispelling stress and assuaging anger, but is also good for any general meditation. Performing this exercise will make it easier for you to perform the meditation suggested by Master Naharo in *The Complete Reiki Course*.

This meditation is performed in a quiet room, or in a quiet place in natural surroundings. For a short while, turn off the radio and the phones, and detach yourself from anything that is liable to disturb you.

1. Prepare yourself for a short meditation. Sit upright on a chair, with your hands on your knees, palms facing upward. Look straight ahead of you. Breathe normally.

2. Empty your consciousness by means of a rhythmic series of inhalations and exhalations. The inhalation rhythm is one-two-three, while the exhalation rhythm is one-two.

3. Relax your muscles from bottom to top. This relaxation is done by contracting the muscle, and then relaxing it completely. Start from the feet, and move up the legs to the abdominal muscles, the chest muscles, the arms, and finally the neck, using light and careful circular movements.

4. Now that your breathing is rhythmic and your body is relaxed, use visualization – that is, display a conscious picture on the "screen" in your mind by means of your imagination – to bring up something that is bothering you, or a picture of someone who has hurt you, or the memory of an aggravating event, or a "karmic" insult that you are dragging behind you. Focus on the "black stain" opposite your eyes, nurture

your anger, "roll" it from right to left, feel your feeling of pain and humiliation once more...

5. While you are trying to amass anger (it's not easy!), turn your hands over so that your palms now face downward. Place your right thumb on your thigh about a hand's width above your right knee, on the inner side, and your right index finger on the parallel point of your thigh on the outer side... and **press** your thigh firmly with your two fingers, pushing your thumb toward your finger. Does it hurt? (After you become familiar with this meditation, you can perform this pressure with both hands on both thighs simultaneously.)

6. Feel the **physical** pain. Continue with the pressure for a few seconds and relax. While the pain is subsiding, imagine it as a dark brown ball held between your knees.

7. Do you remember the anger you amassed (or tried to amass) at the beginning of the meditation? Where is it? You suddenly feel as if this anger has subsided, or has been forgotten, as a result of the sharp pain you caused yourself.

8. Now focus on the anger again (and don't be surprised if you find it difficult to do so, since the anger has "disappeared").

9. Now you must visualize the anger as a dark red ball, which floats opposite your chest (opposite the heart chakra). Imagine that a net made of threads of light is cast downward (from the crown chakra, if you like) and catches the dark red ball of anger. The net pulls the ball **downward**, toward the place where the ball of dark brown physical pain is located, between your knees.

10. Now merge the two balls together. Let the anger penetrate the physical pain and become assimilated inside it, until you only see one ball in your visualization.

11. Take calm, rhythmic meditation breaths (using a one-two-three... one-two rhythm), at the same time pressing the (caught) ball from between your knees into the earth, and causing the anger-pain ball to disappear into the earth.

12. Feel your physical body (you can do this by moving your hands over your legs, for example). Look for the pain and you will find that it has disappeared... and the anger has disappeared in the same way!

13. Come back to full consciousness. Take a few deep breaths before standing up. Shake your limbs and stretch your back.

After this meditation, you can resume your regular everyday activities with redoubled strength.

When you practice this meditation (like any other meditation), you will discover that you can do the whole thing in approximately five minutes, and that you do not need the physical pressure of the fingers in order to feel the physical pain (nor do you need to move your hands over your body, as in stage 12). It is sufficient to visualize the entire process.

Of course, this is just an example of a particular meditation that can be used. The reader who wishes to exploit Reiki energy to the maximum must know methods of meditation and focusing, and practice them regularly. Activating Reiki without meditation to make it flow – in the opinion of some Reiki experts – is just half of the Reiki energy the person needs. In contrast, activating Reiki with meditation (and Reiki symbols) always utilizes the flow of Reiki to the maximum.